The Way

Live Light
Walk Deep

The Soul's Journey Beyond Ego,
Noise and the Need for More

Live Light
Walk Deep

**The Soul's Journey Beyond Ego,
Noise and the Need for More**

Rob Chapman

Copyright © 2025 Rob Chapman. All right reserved.

No part of this book may be reproduced or transmitted in any form whatsoever. Electronically or mechanical, including photocopying, recording, or by informational, storage or retrieval system, without the express written, dated, and signed permission of the author.

ISBN: 9798283017037

Imprint: Independently published

Dedication

For Fee
For your support and love

For Amy

For getting excited about the plan.

For God
Where do I start.

For You

The Reader
Because you are enough.
Be the light in the world.

Content

Introduction	p1
The Call to Live	p5
The Quiet Strength of Humility	p15
The Truth that Transforms	p27
The Wisdom of Thoughtful Action	p39
The Sacred Art of Reading	p49
The Weight of Wanting	p61
The Illusion of Pride	p71
The Company We Keep	p81
The Truth About Obedience	p91
Don't Fill the Silence, Feel It	p99
Feeling Scattered?	P109
When Love Becomes the Reason	p117
The People Who Test Us	p129

Content

A Life Set Apart	p139
The Gift of Withdrawal	p151
Tears That Heal	p159
The Ache You Can't Name	p169
Die Before You Die	p177
What If Struggles	p185
Temptation isn't the Problem	p193
The Habit that's Quietly	p207
The Flame That Once Burned	p219
Living The Inner Vow	p229
The Sacred Reset	p239
Afterward	p247
Recommended Reading	p251
A Blessing	p257

Introduction:

Whispers on the Wind

This book was never meant to be written in loud proclamations.

It began as quiet murmurs—meditations in the margins, reflections born out of lived experience, and gentle conversations with the sacred. Each chapter arose not from dogma, but from a desire to listen more deeply, to live more honestly, and to hold space for the unspoken longings that stir beneath the surface of everyday life.

You will not find rigid theology here. Nor a map for how to be spiritual the 'right' way. Instead, you'll find echoes—of ancient wisdom, of inner awakenings, of moments when the veil thinned and something real broke through.

Much of what follows is inspired by timeless spiritual themes that have endured across centuries, including the writings known as *The Imitation of Christ*—but these pages are not bound to the language or doctrine of their time. They have been reimagined, reframed, and rewritten for the soul who walks the path today: the seeker, the doubter, the mystic-in-the-making.

Celtic Christianity, with its reverence for creation and its embrace of mystery, threads through these pages as a quiet undercurrent. So too does a belief in the goodness of the human soul—its capacity for transformation, and its longing for reunion with the sacred.

This book is part invitation, part offering. A mirror held up not to show you what you lack, but to remind you of what was never lost.

There is no need to read in order. Let your heart guide you. Start where the light enters. Skip, pause, return. These are not lessons to master but companions for your own unfolding.

May these whispers reach you when you need them most.

And may they awaken what is already within.

— Rob

The Call to Live, Not Just Know

We live in an age overflowing with knowledge. Wisdom, advice, and self-improvement techniques are at our fingertips. We can access lectures from world-class scholars, watch endless spiritual talks, and consume information faster than ever before. Yet, despite this, how many of us truly live what we know?

What good is knowing, if it does not change who we are?

This is not a question for scholars or philosophers alone. It speaks directly into our modern world. We admire wisdom but often fail to embody it. We follow inspirational figures, read spiritual books, and share quotes about peace and love—yet, when faced with challenges, do we actually live these truths? Do we meet frustration with gentleness? Do we choose faith over fear?

A World of Knowledge, A Hunger for Wisdom

Social media, podcasts, and online courses offer limitless access to knowledge. But has it made us wiser? Or just more opinionated? Many seek identity in being knowledgeable, forgetting that true wisdom is lived, not learned.

The early Celtic Christian monks understood this well. They didn't sit debating theology in ivory towers. They walked the coasts, tended the land, and lived in rhythm with God. Their faith was not a subject of discussion; it was a way of being. The question remains as relevant today as ever: Are we collecting ideas, or are we letting them transform us?

This difference between knowledge and wisdom has never been starker. We are bombarded with information, yet we are starved of depth. We chase after facts, statistics, and spiritual insights but seldom pause long enough to let them take root in our hearts. There is a quiet arrogance in assuming that simply knowing something means we have mastered it. True wisdom is slow. It takes time. It seeps into our bones through experience, through reflection, through living it.

The Illusion of Importance

There is a danger in the vanity of knowledge for its own sake. Today, this might look like:

Measuring self-worth by achievements or credentials.

Seeking spiritual insights but refusing to surrender pride.

Debating truth rather than living truth.

Amassing knowledge but resisting transformation.

We are conditioned to believe that the more we know, the more we are worth. Intelligence, status, and influence have become markers of value. But the true spiritual path does not reward the most knowledgeable—it rewards the most humble. Those who live their faith quietly, without need for recognition, are the ones who truly walk in wisdom.

This is a difficult truth in a world that thrives on visibility. We want to be seen as wise, enlightened, successful. But the most profound wisdom often grows in hidden places. It is not found in loud declarations or in public debates—it is found in the quiet moment when we choose kindness over judgment, faith over cynicism, humility over self-importance.

Walking the Path, Not Just Talking About It

What does this look like today? It is easy to talk about the need for peace in the world, but do we cultivate peace within ourselves? It is easy to admire those who serve the poor, but do we make space in our own lives to serve? It is easy to quote scripture, but do we embody the teachings?

We do not need more opinions about faith. We need more embodied faith.

Living truth is not always grand or dramatic. Often, it is in the small, unnoticed moments:

Holding your tongue when anger rises.

Offering a kind word to a stranger.

Choosing patience when things don't go your way.

Sitting in silence and listening, rather than rushing to speak.

Each of these moments is an opportunity to move from knowledge to practice, from ideas to embodiment. The spiritual path is not about accumulating more information, but about being willing to be changed by what we already know.

The call is not to accumulate knowledge, but to be changed by it.

The challenge is simple but radical: Live the truth you seek. Not just in words. Not just in what we claim to believe. But in the very way we live, breathe, and move through this world.

Letting Go of the Need to Be Right

One of the greatest obstacles to true wisdom is our attachment to being right. We crave validation. We want to prove our point. We want to be seen as knowledgeable and insightful. But wisdom is not about winning arguments; it is about transformation.

We see this in the way we interact online. How often do discussions become battlegrounds? How often do people enter into conversations not to understand, but to prove their own viewpoint? Even in spiritual circles, people argue over theology, philosophy, and the "correct" way to practice faith. But what does any of this matter if we are not becoming more like Christ?

There is a deep humility in being willing to say: *I do not need to be right. I do not need to win this debate. I only need to walk in love.*

Letting go of the need to be right allows us to listen. It allows us to be soft. It allows us to grow. It allows us to be transformed in ways we could not have imagined if we remained rigidly attached to our own perspective.

An Invitation

Perhaps today is a moment to pause. To shift from seeking knowledge to embodying wisdom. To let go of the need to be right, to be admired, or to be knowledgeable. To simply ask:

How can I live more like Christ today?

This is not about grand gestures. It is about the quiet, unnoticed choices that shape the soul. It is about choosing love when it is difficult, choosing patience when it is inconvenient, choosing faith when the world is uncertain.

The world does not need more people who know about faith. It needs people who embody it.

The Quiet Strength of Humility: Letting Go to Become More

We live in a world that celebrates self-promotion. From social media to career advancement, we are constantly encouraged to stand out, build our brand, and prove our worth. Even in spirituality, there is a subtle pressure to be seen as knowledgeable, wise, or enlightened.

But what if the path to true peace, wisdom, and inner strength lies not in becoming more but in letting go?

Humility is often misunderstood. It is not about thinking less of ourselves, but rather thinking beyond ourselves. It is a freedom from the exhausting need to be admired, validated, or in control.

At its core, humility is a way of moving through the world lightly, without the weight of self-importance. It allows us to see more clearly, listen more deeply, and love more freely.

It is not weakness. It is liberation.

The Heavy Burden of Self-Importance

We are subtly trained to build our identity on what we know, what we achieve, and how others perceive us. But the more we depend on these things, the more fragile we become.

- If our confidence is built on always being right, we become defensive and closed to learning.

- If our worth is tied to success, we live in constant anxiety of failure.
- If we seek recognition, we are always at the mercy of other people's opinions.

And yet, we hold onto these things because they give us a false sense of security. We believe that if we can just prove ourselves, then we will finally feel worthy.

But self-importance is a heavy thing to carry. It keeps us restless, striving, and never at peace.

This is why humility is the greatest act of self-liberation.

It is not self-denial—it is self-transcendence. It allows us to step off the exhausting treadmill of proving ourselves and instead find rest in something greater than our own importance.

The Wisdom of the Humble

The Celtic spiritual tradition has long understood the quiet power of humility.

In ancient Ireland and Scotland, wisdom was not found in grand debates, public recognition, or status. It was found in those who listened more than they spoke, who walked gently upon the land, and who sought to live in harmony with the unseen rhythms of life.

The Celtic monks, much like the Desert Fathers before them, embraced lives of simplicity, service, and surrender. They left behind positions of power, choosing instead to live close to the earth and close to God.

They understood something that modern culture often forgets:

- **The strongest trees bend with the wind, rather than resisting it.**

- **The clearest waters are found in the stillest places.**
- **The greatest wisdom is often unspoken.**

To be humble is not to be small, but to be steady—unshaken by the changing tides of public opinion or personal pride.

What Humility is Not

Humility is not thinking you are worthless. It is not erasing yourself or pretending you have nothing to offer.

It is simply knowing that your worth is not dependent on comparison, success, or approval. It is recognizing that you do not have to be the centre of everything to have value.

Many people resist humility because they think it means losing themselves. But in truth, humility is where we find ourselves—not in striving, but in surrender.

The Art of Letting Go

The path of humility is a path of releasing what weighs us down.

- **Let go of the need to be seen.** Your value is not measured by attention or applause.

- **Let go of the need to be right.** Peace is found in openness, not in winning arguments.

- **Let go of comparison.** Another person's success does not diminish your own.

- **Let go of control.** The world does not revolve around your efforts alone.

Humility is the art of holding life lightly, trusting that we are already held by something far greater than our own strength.

The Freedom of the Humble

Humility does not mean passivity. It does not mean giving up. It means choosing peace over pride, openness over defensiveness, and surrender over struggle.

- **The humble do not fear being overlooked.** They know their worth is not dependent on visibility.

- **The humble do not need to be right.** They are more interested in truth than in winning debates.

- **The humble are free from comparison.** They celebrate

others' success rather than resent it.

And most importantly—the humble are at peace.

Because they have nothing to prove. Nothing to defend. Nothing to chase.

They are already enough.

Living Humility in the Modern World

In a world that tells us to seek status, recognition, and influence, how do we walk the path of humility?

1. Choose Silence Over Noise

The loudest voice is not always the wisest. In a world of constant opinions, practice listening more than you speak.

2. Serve Without Seeking Credit

Do something good today—without telling anyone about it.

3. Accept That You Don't Have to Have All the Answers

It's okay to say, "I don't know." There is wisdom in admitting our limitations.

4. Let Go of Defensiveness

Not every disagreement is a battle that must be won. Sometimes, the most powerful response is graceful silence.

5. Practice Letting Others Shine

Resist the urge to compete. Celebrate someone else's achievements without feeling diminished.

6. Be Present, Not Perfect

Humility allows us to embrace the imperfect, to be real rather than impressive.

7. Find Strength in Something Greater Than Yourself

The humble are not weak—they are deeply rooted. When you know that your worth is not dependent on external validation, you become unshakable.

The Sacred Relief of Humility

Imagine the relief of not needing to prove yourself. Imagine the freedom of letting go of comparison, self-importance, and control.

Imagine waking up each morning and knowing that your worth is not something you have to earn—it simply is.

Humility is not a loss of self—it is a return to our true self, the self that is not driven by fear, but by love.

It is a surrender, not to weakness, but to wisdom.

It is an invitation to breathe, to let go, and to trust that we are already enough.

The Truth That Transforms: Walking the Path, Not Just Studying the Map

We live in an age of endless knowledge. Answers are at our fingertips, available at any moment. We consume books, podcasts, documentaries, and discussions, all in pursuit of greater understanding.

But for all this knowledge, are we any wiser?

Do we live differently because of what we know? Or do we simply collect information, mistaking accumulation for transformation?

There is a difference between knowing about something and embodying it. True wisdom is not found in gathering ideas, but in living truthfully.

The Difference Between Knowing and Living

Imagine standing at the edge of a vast forest, holding a beautifully detailed map. The map tells you where the rivers flow, where the steep climbs are, and where the best resting places lie.

You could study that map for hours, memorizing every path and every landmark.

But unless you step into the forest and walk the path yourself, you will never truly know it.

The modern world is filled with map-readers—those who collect knowledge, analyse, debate, and discuss—but fewer are walkers of the path.

Knowledge without practice is like holding a map you never use.

- You can read every book on love, but it will never teach you how to love another human being in the hardest moments of life.

- You can learn about forgiveness, but until you forgive someone who has deeply hurt you, you won't truly understand it.

- You can talk about faith, but it is only in walking through uncertainty and surrendering control that faith becomes real.

Celtic Christianity: The Embodied Path of Truth

The Celtic spiritual tradition does not separate knowing from living. It teaches that wisdom is something we do, not just something we learn.

The early monks and seekers of the Celtic lands understood that truth is woven into creation itself—not just in sacred texts or philosophical debates, but in the land, in stillness, in experience. They learned truth from the waves against the shore, the turning of the seasons, the way fire gives warmth but also destroys.

For them, faith was not an abstract concept—it was a lived reality, something as real as the wind on their faces or the ground beneath their feet.

This is why many of them became wanderers, setting out without destinations, trusting that the path itself would shape them. They did not just talk about trust in God—they walked into the unknown and lived it.

Their wisdom can be summed up in a simple but radical question:

Is your faith something you know, or something you live?

The Modern Search for Meaning

Today, we are drowning in more information than ever before. We consume podcasts, self-help books, spiritual teachings, and courses—yet anxiety, burnout, and disconnection are at an all-time high.

Why?

Because information does not equal transformation.

Many of us mistake learning about something for becoming it. We believe that if we just read more, we will become wiser. If we just listen to the right voices, we will be more grounded.

But truth is not found in more information—it is found in how we embody what we already know.

- We know that being present is important, yet we spend our days distracted.

- We know that rest is necessary, yet we push ourselves to exhaustion.

- We know that kindness is powerful, yet we hold onto grievances.

So the real challenge is not learning more—it is living what we already know.

Why We Resist Living the Truth

If transformation is found in walking the path, why do so many of us resist it?

Because living truthfully requires surrender.

- It requires letting go of control, rather than clinging to certainty.
- It requires risk, because real wisdom is often uncomfortable.
- It requires humility, because it means admitting we have to change.

It is easier to talk about truth than to let it shape us. It is easier to study love than to practice it when it's hard.

But wisdom is not gained in comfort. It is gained in stepping forward when we don't have all the answers.

How Do We Begin to Walk the Path?

If we want to shift from knowing truth to living it, we must make it part of our everyday lives.

Here are some ways to do that:

1. Slow Down and Listen

The Celts believed that truth is not just learned—it is discovered in stillness.

- Spend time in silence each day.
- Listen to the quiet wisdom that already exists inside you.
- Notice where truth is already present in your life.

2. Live Simply

Truth is often lost in distraction, busyness, and complexity.

- Ask: What is unnecessary in my life? What is keeping me from clarity?
- Let go of excess noise, whether it's too much media, too many opinions, or too many commitments.
- Return to what is essential—things that bring life, not just stimulation.

3. Take One Step at a Time

Transformation does not happen all at once. It happens in small, daily choices.

- Instead of trying to change everything, choose one thing you know is true and live it today.
- If you know rest is important, commit to resting fully without guilt.

- If you know honesty is powerful, speak with integrity, even in small conversations.

4. Let Go of the Need to Be Right

Truth is not about proving ourselves. It is about becoming more aligned with wisdom.

- Be open to learning from unexpected places.
- Practice deep listening rather than preparing a response.
- Let go of needing to be right, and instead focus on understanding more deeply.

5. Trust That the Path Will Shape You

The early Celtic wanderers stepped into the unknown, trusting that walking would teach them what they could not learn by standing still.

- You do not need to have all the answers before you begin.
- Trust that by living the truth—even when it's hard, even when it's uncertain—you will be shaped in ways you could never have planned.

Truth Is Meant to Be Lived

Perhaps today is a call to stop seeking more knowledge and start living more truthfully.

Because wisdom is not found in what we know—it is found in how we walk through the world.

Truth is waiting.

Not in the next book. Not in the next conversation.

But in the choices you make today.

The Wisdom of Thoughtful Action: Choosing Discernment Over Impulse

We live in a world of instant reactions. News spreads in seconds, opinions are shared without reflection, and judgment is often made before the full picture is revealed. The ability to pause, reflect, and act with wisdom is increasingly rare—but it is also one of the most powerful skills we can cultivate.

What if wisdom is not found in knowing everything, but in knowing when to listen, when to speak, and when to remain still?

The Danger of Acting Without Thought

Modern culture celebrates speed and decisiveness. We are told to trust our instincts, respond quickly, and always have an opinion. But as history and personal experience show, many of our worst decisions come from reacting too soon.

How many times have we:

- Jumped to conclusions about a person, only to realize later we misjudged them?

- Spoken out of anger and regretted the words that could never be taken back?

- Believed gossip without questioning its truth?

- Made a major life decision without seeking counsel, only to later wish we had waited?

True wisdom is not about having immediate answers—it is about knowing when to pause, when to seek guidance, and when to trust silence.

Celtic Wisdom: The Strength of Stillness

In Celtic spirituality, wisdom is not found in impulsive reactions but in a deep, steady awareness of life's rhythms. The early monks and seekers of Ireland and Scotland did not rush to speak, act, or judge. Instead, they cultivated discernment—the ability to see clearly, wait patiently, and act intentionally.

They understood that:

- Words hold power—they can heal or wound, unite or divide.
- Not all information is truth—some is distorted, exaggerated, or incomplete.
- True wisdom comes from humility—from seeking guidance rather than assuming we know best.

Their approach was not one of inaction, but of deliberate action. They did not avoid speaking or acting, but they chose when and how to do so with great care.

The Trap of Gossip and Assumptions

One of the greatest dangers of acting without discernment is our tendency to believe and repeat what we hear without question.

- How often do we hear a piece of gossip and assume it must be true?
- How often do we judge someone based on a single moment rather than their whole character?
- How often do we form opinions without seeking full understanding?

It is far easier to believe the worst in others than to seek the truth. But true wisdom requires that we:

- Do not believe everything we hear. Truth is often more complex than the first story we are told.

- Do not repeat everything we hear. Just because something is believed does not mean it must be shared.

- Seek understanding before forming opinions. Take time to reflect before deciding what is true.

The Power of Seeking Counsel

One of the greatest marks of wisdom is knowing that we do not know everything. The wisest people are not those who rely only on themselves, but those who seek guidance from others.

- Who do you turn to for wisdom?

- Do you surround yourself with people who challenge and refine your thinking?

- Are you open to advice, or do you resist correction?

The ancient Celts understood the power of wise counsel. They did not live in isolation but formed communities of wisdom—learning from elders, mentors, and spiritual guides.

They knew that:

- A wise friend sees what we cannot see.
- A humble heart is willing to learn.
- The more we listen, the less we regret.

The Humility of Waiting

One of the hardest disciplines of wisdom is learning to wait.

- Waiting before speaking in anger.
- Waiting before making a decision.

- Waiting before passing judgment.

The world pressures us to act now, speak now, decide now. But the greatest decisions in life often require patience, prayer, and thoughtful reflection.

The more we practice waiting, the less we will regret.

Living with Wisdom in Everyday Life

How can we cultivate wisdom and forethought in our daily lives?

1 Pause Before Reacting

- Before responding to an email, a comment, or an insult, take a breath.
- Ask yourself: Am I reacting or responding?

2 Think Before Speaking

- Not every thought needs to be voiced.
- Choose words that build up rather than tear down.

3 Question What You Hear

- Just because something is said does not mean it is true.
- Take time to seek full understanding before forming an opinion.

4 Seek Wise Counsel

- Do not make major decisions alone.
- Surround yourself with people who will challenge and refine you.

5 Practice Humility

- Accept that you do not have all the answers.

- Be willing to admit when you are wrong and learn from others.

The Peace of a Thoughtful Life

When we act with wisdom and forethought, we live with fewer regrets. We are no longer at the mercy of impulsive decisions, thoughtless words, and hasty judgments.

Instead, we live with clarity, purpose, and peace—moving through the world with intention rather than reaction.

Perhaps today is a call to pause, reflect, and listen—to seek wisdom rather than impulse.

Because a life built on thoughtful, intentional action is a life that leaves no room for regret.

The Sacred Art of Reading: Receiving Wisdom Instead of Seeking Status

In an age of constant information, we often consume knowledge rather than absorb wisdom. We read to be informed, to debate, to impress others with our understanding—but how often do we read to be transformed?

What if reading was not about what we know, but who we become because of it?

In both ancient Celtic wisdom and spiritual traditions across the world, reading was never just about gathering facts—it was a sacred act, a way of entering into something larger than oneself. The words we take in shape us, not just intellectually, but at the deepest levels of our soul.

The Illusion of Intellectual Pride

Modern culture celebrates those who speak the most, know the most, and debate the best. We have built a world where knowledge is often used as a weapon—to prove superiority, to outsmart, to impress.

But knowledge alone is empty if it does not change us.

The Celtic Christian tradition emphasized humility in learning. Reading was approached reading as a form of prayer, not as an intellectual contest. They understood that:

- The greatest wisdom is often found in simplicity.
- Reading with humility opens the heart to transformation.
- Truth is not about who said it, but what is being said.

In contrast, today we often ask:

- *Who wrote this? (Do they have authority?)*
- *How does this align with my current views? (Can I use this to confirm what I already believe?)*
- *How does this make me look? (Can I use this knowledge to impress others?)*

But true wisdom asks only one thing:

What is the truth here, and how can I live it?

Reading as a Path to Transformation

There is a vast difference between reading to know and reading to be changed.

- The first seeks control—
  to master ideas.
- The second seeks surrender—
  to be mastered by wisdom.

We have all read things that have stayed with us for years—not because they gave us new facts, but because they shifted something deep inside us.

The Celts believed that the spoken and written word carried power—that words were not just symbols on a page, but living things capable of shaping the world.

If this is true, then how we read matters just as much as what we read.

Why Do We Read?

- Do we read to seek deeper truth—or just to confirm our existing beliefs?
- Do we read with humility—or with the desire to prove ourselves?
- Do we read to be transformed—or to accumulate knowledge?

The difference between spiritual reading and intellectual consumption is simple:

- Spiritual reading invites us to listen—it is an act of receiving, not just analysing.
- Intellectual reading invites us to argue—it is an act of mastering knowledge, rather than letting it master us.

One leads to wisdom. The other often leads to arrogance.

Letting Go of the Need to Debate

One of the greatest obstacles to deep understanding is the desire to dissect and debate rather than listen.

- How often do we interrupt our reading with scepticism, argument, or resistance?
- How often do we reject wisdom from unexpected places, because it doesn't fit into our existing framework?

The ancient Celts had a phrase:

"Listen twice before speaking once."

This applied not only to conversation, but to reading and receiving wisdom.

Rather than asking:
"Do I agree with this?"

They would ask:
"What is this teaching me?"

This shift in mindset changes everything.

Humility in Learning

True wisdom does not seek to win—it seeks to understand.

The greatest teachers are those who:

- Read with openness, rather than resistance.
- Ask questions, rather than assume answers.
- Let wisdom shape them, rather than trying to control it.

There is a sacred relief in humility—in not needing to be the expert, prove ourselves, or have all the answers.

The world is filled with voices clamouring to be heard. But the truly wise are those who listen, absorb, and let truth settle deep into their being.

How to Read for Wisdom, Not Just Knowledge

So how do we shift from reading for status to reading for transformation?

1. Read With an Open Heart

Instead of reading to confirm what you already believe, read to be challenged and expanded.

- Let go of the need to defend yourself against new ideas.
- Approach words with curiosity, rather than resistance.

- Assume there is something to learn in every experience.

2. Do Not Dismiss Based on the Source

We often judge wisdom by who said it rather than what is being said.

- Truth is not owned by any one person, culture, or belief system.
- A humble teacher may reveal more than a celebrated expert.
- Do not let your pride prevent you from receiving wisdom.

3. Read Slowly, Read Thoughtfully

The ancient Celts valued slow, meditative reading—not rushing through texts, but sitting with them, allowing them to sink in.

Try this:

- Instead of racing to finish a book, pause and reflect on one idea at a time.
- Ask: *How does this apply to my life?*
- Let go of the pressure to "get through" knowledge—wisdom is not measured in pages read.

4. Ask Questions, Then Be Still

Wisdom is often revealed in quiet, rather than debate.

- Instead of arguing with the text, sit with it.
- Ask: *What is this teaching me?*
- Then, be silent. Let the answer come in its own time.

5. Seek Truth, Not Just Information

Not everything that sounds impressive is meaningful.

- Do not chase complexity for its own sake—often, the most simple truths are the deepest.
- Ask: *Does this lead me toward greater love, wisdom, and peace?*
- If the answer is yes, hold onto it. If not, let it go.

Reading as a Spiritual Practice

What if reading was not just a way to consume information, but a way to connect to something greater?

What if it was an act of stillness, humility, and transformation—rather than a race to know more, be right, or impress others?

The Celtic monks saw reading as a form of prayer—a time to sit with wisdom, to listen deeply, to let truth unfold in the heart.

What if we returned to this way of learning?

Perhaps today is an invitation—to read not to conquer knowledge, but to be changed by it.

Because in the end, it is not what we know that matters.

It is who we become because of it.

The Weight of Wanting: Finding Peace Beyond Desire

We live in a world that tells us to want more, seek more, achieve more. Advertisements tell us that happiness is just one more purchase away. Social media fuels the idea that we should always be striving for something better—a better career, a better relationship, a better version of ourselves.

But what if the very act of wanting more is what keeps us from peace?

What if true contentment is not in getting what we desire, but in learning to let go of the need to have it in the first place?

The Restlessness of Desire

There is a pattern to how desire works.

We want something—a promotion, a new experience, recognition, material comfort.

We tell ourselves that once we have it, we will be satisfied.

If we don't get it, we feel frustrated, restless, or resentful.

If we do get it, the satisfaction doesn't last, and soon we are chasing something new.

The cycle never ends.

Ancient wisdom teaches that desire itself is not the problem—it is disordered desire that causes suffering.

Wanting good things is natural, but when we seek them above all else, we become trapped.

The proud and greedy never find rest, because they are always seeking more.

The humble and content find peace, because they are not constantly grasping for what they do not have.

This is not about rejecting joy or living in denial—it is about learning the difference between what truly satisfies the soul and what only provides temporary pleasure.

Celtic Wisdom: The Power of Simplicity

The Celtic monks and seekers of Ireland and Britain understood this well. They lived simply , walked the land as wanderers, and sought God in stillness and solitude. They were not concerned with accumulating wealth, power, or recognition—they were concerned with freeing the soul from attachment to worldly things.

They believed:

- True peace is not found in having more, but in needing less.
- The quieter the life, the louder the voice of the Spirit.
- Happiness is not found in external things, but in the state of the heart.

They chose a life of simplicity, not because they had to, but because they recognized that the more they owned, the more owned them.

This is a truth that still applies today.

The less we are consumed by wanting, the freer we are to live fully in the present moment.

The less we chase after things, the more peace we find in what we already have.

The Struggle of Letting Go

But letting go of desire is hard.

If we stop chasing, what will be left?

If we give up what we think we need, will we still be happy?

This is where many people struggle. They may try to detach from worldly things, but instead of finding peace, they feel empty, sad, or even resentful.

Why?

Because desire does not disappear overnight.

The mind is conditioned to seek fulfilment in external things. When those things are removed, the emptiness feels unbearable.

But that emptiness is the beginning of transformation.

Instead of reaching for the next distraction, we are invited to sit with the discomfort, to question our cravings, to examine what truly nourishes us.

The Illusion of Getting What We Want

Have you ever wanted something desperately—a new opportunity, a material possession, a person's approval—only to finally get it and realize it didn't bring the peace you expected?

That's because peace was never in the thing itself.

Peace is not in the money we make, but in how we relate to what we have.

Peace is not in how people see us, but in how we see ourselves.

Peace is not in controlling our circumstances, but in trusting that we are held, even in uncertainty.

When we resist desire, rather than being controlled by it, we open the door to a deeper kind of contentment—one that is not dependent on external conditions.

How to Break Free from the Cycle of Desire

If inordinate desires make us restless, then how do we reclaim inner peace?

Here are five ways to begin:

1. Pause Before Acting on Desire

The next time you feel a strong craving—for a new possession, for validation, for something you believe you *must* have—pause.

Ask: *Will this bring lasting peace, or is this just temporary relief?*

2. Practice Gratitude for What Already Exists

Contentment is not found in getting more, but in appreciating what is already here.

Shift your focus: Instead of asking *What do I lack?* ask *What do I already have that brings joy, peace, or fulfilment?*

3. Be Honest About What Truly Satisfies You

The things we chase often provide only surface-level satisfaction.

Reflect: *What has brought me the deepest fulfilment in life?* (Hint: It's rarely material things.)

4. Embrace Simplicity

Less is often more. Consider simplifying your environment, your commitments, and your expectations.

Let go of things that add stress rather than joy.

5. Shift Your Focus to Something Greater

True peace is found not in running after desires, but in aligning ourselves with something deeper—whether that be faith, love, service, or inner stillness.

Instead of focusing on what you want, focus on who you are becoming.

A Life That Is Light and Free

Imagine a life where you no longer feel weighed down by wanting.

Where you can enjoy the beauty of life without needing to cling to it.

Where you feel at peace even when you don't have everything you desire.

Where you are no longer chasing fulfilment, because you have found it within yourself.

This is the gift of letting go.

This is the path of true freedom.

Perhaps today is an invitation to release the weight of wanting, to step out of the cycle of always needing more, and to discover that peace is not something we chase—it is something we allow.

Because in the end, what we let go of may be exactly what sets us free.

The Illusion of Pride: Finding Strength in Humility

We live in a world where status, power, and self-reliance are often seen as the keys to success. We are taught to trust in our own abilities, to take pride in our achievements, and to build security in wealth, reputation, or influence.

But what if the very things we rely on—our strength, intelligence, beauty, or status—are the things that make us most vulnerable?

What if true security is not found in what we build for ourselves, but in what we surrender?

Ancient wisdom teaches us that pride isolates, while humility frees. The more we seek to exalt ourselves, the more fragile our sense of worth becomes. But the more we learn to trust in something beyond ourselves, the lighter and freer we are to truly live.

The Trap of Placing Trust in Ourselves

Pride is often subtle. It isn't always about arrogance or superiority—it can also be the quiet belief that we must be entirely self-sufficient.

We place trust in:

- Our achievements—believing that if we just accomplish enough, we will be fulfilled.
- Our wealth or possessions—thinking that security comes from what we own.

- Our status and reputation—fearing that if we lose the respect of others, we will lose ourselves.
- Our intelligence and talents—believing that our worth is tied to how skilled or knowledgeable we are.

But all these things fade, fail, or shift.

Success is temporary—there is always something more to achieve.

Wealth can disappear overnight—possessions can never guarantee peace.

Physical beauty declines—no one can outrun time.

Reputation is fragile—what people think of us today may change tomorrow.

The ancient Celts understood this truth well. They did not measure strength by outward power but by the depth of one's spirit. They knew that real security does not come from what we have, but from how we live.

The Humility of the Celtic Saints

In Celtic Christianity, humility is not seen as weakness, but as a way of being free from the weight of self-importance.

The Irish and British saints often rejected positions of influence, choosing instead to live as wanderers, hermits, or simple servants. Their strength was not in their titles, achievements, or wealth, but in their willingness to let go of everything and trust fully in God.

They believed:

- Relying on oneself brings anxiety; relying on the Divine brings peace.

- The more we seek to prove our worth, the less we recognize our inherent value.
- True power is not found in control, but in surrender.

This is why many Celtic monks took vows of poverty and service, not out of self-denial, but because they knew that the more we let go, the more we gain.

The Cost of Pride

Pride is a heavy burden to carry.

It makes us compare ourselves to others, fuelling jealousy and resentment.

It creates fear of failure, because our identity is tied to being the best.

It isolates us, because we feel we must maintain an image rather than admit our struggles.

The world rewards those who are self-made, independent, and proud—but at what cost?

The proud are often:

Restless—because their security is fragile.

Anxious—because they fear losing what they have built.

Lonely—because their worth is tied to being admired, rather than being real.

On the other hand, humility frees us.

The humble person is not weighed down by status.

They do not need to prove themselves.

They find peace in knowing that they are enough—without striving, without comparison, without fear.

Letting Go of the Need to Be More

So how do we step out of the trap of pride and self-reliance?

Here are five ways to cultivate humility and find true freedom:

1. Stop Measuring Yourself by External Standards

You are not your achievements, your wealth, or your reputation.

Your worth does not rise or fall based on what others think.

Ask yourself: *If I lost everything I take pride in, who would I be?*

2. Learn to Serve Without Expectation

Celtic monks saw service as a way of dismantling the ego.

Do small acts of kindness without recognition—help someone, give anonymously, listen deeply.

True service is done without needing anything in return.

3. Trust in Something Greater Than Yourself

You do not have to hold everything together alone.

Let go of the belief that your value is in what you control.

Surrender the need to be self-sufficient—true strength comes from connection, not isolation.

4. See Others as Equals, Not Competitors

Do not look at what others have and feel less than or greater than—just see them as fellow travellers.

Instead of asking, *Am I better than them?*, ask *How can I learn from them?*

Celebrate others' successes without comparison or envy.

5. Accept That You Are Already Enough

You do not need to prove your worth—you were already worthy the moment you existed.

True peace comes not from climbing higher, but from stepping off the ladder altogether.

Ask: *What would my life look like if I no longer needed to impress anyone—including myself?*

The Freedom of Humility

Imagine a life where you no longer have to seek approval, defend your worth, or compete for success.

Where you can rest, knowing that you are enough.

Where your happiness is not tied to external things.

Where you are free to serve, love, and live fully without fear of failure.

This is the freedom of humility.

Perhaps today is a call to let go of self-importance, to release the fear of losing status, and to step into a life of peace, trust, and true strength.

Because in the end, the greatest power is not in exalting ourselves, but in realizing we never had to.

The Company We Keep: The Power of Boundaries in a Noisy World

In an age of constant connection, we are surrounded by people—both in-person and online. Social media gives us instant access to countless opinions, influencers, and conversations. We are encouraged to network widely, be open, share our thoughts freely, and form as many connections as possible.

But is being constantly connected the same as being deeply known?

Ancient wisdom warns us that not every connection is beneficial. The people we spend time with shape our thoughts, our emotions, and even our spiritual well-being. While we are called to love all people, we are not meant to give everyone unlimited access to our hearts.

The question is not "How many people do I know?" but "Who do I allow to truly influence me?"

The Illusion of Social Closeness

We live in an era where friendships are measured in likes and follows. The more connections we have, the more valuable we feel.

We overshare online, mistaking digital intimacy for true trust.

We allow too many voices into our inner world, confusing opinions with wisdom.

We assume that closeness equals authenticity, forgetting that some connections weaken us rather than strengthen us.

But real relationships are not built on proximity, access, or shared space—they are built on trust, wisdom, and alignment of values.

Ancient Celtic spirituality recognized this deeply. The Celtic monks and hermits were not isolationists, but they understood that not every connection is life-giving. They surrounded themselves with the humble, the simple, and the wise, avoiding distractions that pulled them away from inner clarity and divine focus.

What if the modern world's obsession with constant connection is actually leaving us more distracted, drained, and disconnected from what truly matters?

The Company We Keep Shapes Us

There's a simple truth: The people we spend time with influence who we become.

If we are surrounded by the anxious, we absorb their fear.

If we spend time with the superficial, we become restless for validation.

If we keep company with the wise, we are shaped by wisdom.

Celtic monastic communities were built on shared devotion, not social status. These spiritual kinships were centred around mutual trust, learning, and a life of faith, where individuals sought guidance from those who embodied wisdom rather than worldly power.

By contrast, modern friendships are often built on convenience, entertainment, or surface-level interactions.

Ask yourself:

- Are my closest relationships deepening my character or distracting me from who I want to become?
- Do the people I surround myself with challenge me to grow, or encourage me to stay comfortable?
- Do I feel more at peace, or more restless, after spending time with them?

Not every relationship is meant to be deep, open, or lifelong. There is wisdom in choosing who we allow close to us.

The Danger of Overexposure

There is also a warning here about sharing too much, too quickly.

In an attempt to be open and transparent, we sometimes reveal too much to the wrong people.

We assume that everyone will value our honesty, but not all ears are safe places for our deepest thoughts.

We overshare personal struggles, hoping for support, only to be met with judgment or gossip.

Ancient wisdom teaches that vulnerability is sacred—it should be given wisely and intentionally, not casually or impulsively.

This doesn't mean we should be closed off, cold, or distrusting—it simply means that not everyone deserves access to the deepest parts of our lives.

Modern Boundaries: Learning When to Step Back

So, in a world that tells us to be everywhere, connect constantly, and share everything, how do we reclaim wisdom in relationships?

1. Choose Depth Over Quantity

Having many acquaintances is not the same as having true friends.

Prioritize deep, meaningful relationships over surface-level interactions.

Less noise, more wisdom.

2. Be Mindful of Oversharing

Not every thought, struggle, or dream needs to be shared publicly or immediately.

Take time to discern who truly listens with care and who simply wants access to your story.

Share your heart with those who protect and respect it.

3. Surround Yourself with Those Who Strengthen You

Ask: *Who makes me more thoughtful, peaceful, or spiritually grounded?*

Choose friendships based on character, not just shared interests.

Be intentional about who you let influence your thoughts and emotions.

4. Don't Chase the Approval of the Powerful

The world tells us to seek status, influence, and recognition.

But true wisdom says: "Do not flatter the rich or seek the company of the great."

Stay close to the humble, the kind, and the wise—not just those with worldly power.

5. Seek Solitude When Needed

Constant social interaction is not always healthy.

Take time to retreat, reflect, and listen to your own soul.

Silence is a gift—use it to reconnect with what truly matters.

Finding Freedom in Fewer, Deeper Connections

Imagine a life where:

You no longer feel the pressure to impress or perform.

Your relationships are genuine, deep, and soul-nourishing.

You are surrounded by people who lift you, rather than drain you.

This is the freedom of choosing relationships wisely.

Perhaps today is a call to step back from noise, from unnecessary exposure, and from shallow interactions—and instead, invest in deeper, truer connections.

Because in the end, the relationships that matter aren't the ones with the most attention, but the ones with the most meaning.

The Truth About Obedience (And Why It's Not What You Think)

In our modern world, freedom is sacred. We prize autonomy, personal choice, and the right to define our own lives. Words like obedience and submission can feel outdated—if not outright oppressive. They seem to belong to a time when hierarchies ruled and individuality was suppressed.

But what if we've misunderstood them?

What if true freedom isn't about always having our own way, but about letting go of our constant need to be in control?

Celtic Wisdom and the Dance of Surrender

The early Celtic Christians knew something we often forget: life has rhythm, and learning to live well means learning to move in harmony with it. This includes knowing when to lead and when to follow, when to speak and when to listen, and above all, when to let go of our will for the sake of a deeper peace.

Obedience, in this sense, wasn't about domination—it was about alignment. Not suppression, but surrender to something wiser than the self.

In many Celtic monastic communities, obedience was an act of love, humility, and shared purpose. It meant trusting in the wisdom of the collective, of the Rule, of the abbot, and of God. It was seen not as a restriction, but as a liberation from ego and restlessness.

Why Modern Individualism Can Feel So Heavy

Our culture teaches us to value choice, preference, and personal freedom above all else. But with that comes a hidden cost:

- Constantly needing to make decisions
- Feeling pressure to get it right on your own
- Resisting advice because you fear looking weak
- Seeing others' authority as a threat to your autonomy

We carry the heavy burden of always needing to be in charge, right, and in control.

But the paradox is this: we are most free when we no longer need to get our way.

Obedience as a Path to Inner Peace

To modern ears, "obedience" sounds like subservience. But when rooted in love and humility, obedience is actually a way of disentangling ourselves from pride and striving.

It teaches us to:

- Yield for the sake of peace, not because we are powerless, but because we are wise.
- Release the need to always assert our opinion, and instead trust in a greater harmony.
- Follow the guidance of others when it's helpful, without feeling diminished.

The spiritual practice of obedience asks:

Can I let go of my agenda, my preferences, my defensiveness—for the sake of love, unity, and peace?

Not out of fear. Not because someone is forcing you. But because your soul is learning to trust the stillness that comes from surrender.

Practical Obedience in the 21st Century

Here are five reflections for bringing the ancient path of humble obedience into the rhythm of modern life:

1. Release the Need to Win Every Discussion

You can be right—and still choose peace. You can hold truth—and still choose silence.

Not every conversation needs a victor.
Sometimes, yielding is the wisest act.

2. Listen More Than You Speak

Practice listening with the intent to understand, not just to respond.
Even if you disagree, make space for other voices. Wisdom often hides in unexpected places.

3. Submit Your Plans to Something Bigger

You don't need to carry everything alone.
Surrender your agenda to God, to wisdom, to trusted community, and ask: *Is this truly right?*
Obedience means saying yes to a path greater than personal gain.

4. Trust Wise Leadership

Whether it's a mentor, a spiritual director, a community elder, or a team leader—

honour the wisdom of those who lead with integrity and humility.
Let yourself be led when it's right to do so.

5. Let Go of Restlessness

We are often tempted by the idea that peace lies elsewhere—in a new place, new project, or new community.
But as this chapter reminds us:

"Though thou run hither and thither, thou wilt not find peace, save in humble subjection."

Peace comes not from change, but from being truly rooted where you are, with a heart that is surrendered and at rest.

The Deep Wisdom of Yielding

This isn't about blind obedience. It's not about letting others misuse their power.

It's about choosing to let go of our grip on self-importance, and trusting the sacred flow of life and love.

When obedience is entered into freely, from love and humility, it becomes a path to:

- Unity over division
- Clarity over confusion
- Stillness over striving
- Freedom over fear

Perhaps today, the invitation is not to fight harder—but to let go more.

To stop running, and finally come to rest.

To listen.

To trust.

To yield.

To be free.

Don't Fill the Silence- Feel It: What Sacred Speech Really Means

We live in a world that never stops speaking.

Voices rise from screens, scrolls, and feeds. Notifications interrupt silence before it can settle.
Conversation is constant. Talking is expected. Silence feels awkward, even suspect.

But beneath the clatter, a question waits: What is the cost of all this noise?

Why We Fill the Silence

Not all conversation is bad.
Some words bring comfort, insight,
belonging. We speak to connect, to share
joy, to lighten the load of a heavy day.
But much of our speech is different—
frantic, empty, habitual.

We talk because we're uncomfortable.
Because we want to belong.
Because the silence might show us
something about ourselves we're not
quite ready to face.

We speak without grounding.
We speak to fill the space.

And so we miss the invitation in the
silence—the whisper beneath the noise.

The Celtic Saints and the Reverence for Speech

In early Celtic Christianity, silence wasn't just the absence of sound—it was the presence of something sacred.

Saints like Brigid, Cuthbert, and Kevin of Glendalough understood that the space between words mattered just as much as the words themselves.
They spent hours in solitude, in prayer, in listening—not because they rejected the world, but because they wanted to speak from a deeper place when they returned to it.

To speak without silence was to risk losing one's centre.

In the *Rule of St. Columbanus*, monks were advised to "guard their lips as they would their hearts." Words were considered tools of either healing or harm. Casual, careless speech was not just seen as a distraction—it was a spiritual danger.

The Wound of Superfluous Words

We often walk away from long conversations feeling drained rather than fed.
Not because of what was said—but because of what was missed:

The moment when we could have simply listened

The choice to be still rather than fill the space

The deeper truth that was lost beneath cleverness or comfort

Even when conversations are good-natured, too much can cloud the soul.

We feel the ache of a connection not quite made, a presence not quite kept.

"Many a time I wish that I had held my peace," says the old text. (*Thomas A. Kempis*)
Not from shame, but from recognition: silence would have brought more peace than speech.

Not All Speech Is Equal

The soul doesn't need noise.
It needs truth, beauty, and stillness.

And these are rarely found in constant chatter.

Words born from rest, prayer, and listening carry a different weight.
They do not fill space—they deepen it.
They do not scatter—they gather.
They do not control—they bless.

This is why the Celtic monks would often pray before speaking, even in company. Their words weren't for performance—they were for peace.

The Practice of Holy Conversation

There is a kind of speech that brings life.

It happens when hearts are quiet.
When egos step aside.
When what is said is anchored in Spirit, not in striving.

This is what Thomas à Kempis points to—not an avoidance of people, but an awareness of the inner cost of casual talk.
When we speak without listening first—to God, to our soul, to the moment—we often miss the truth.

But when we allow our words to rise slowly, like incense, they become acts of worship.

How to Speak Like a Celtic Saint in the 21st Century

Here are some practices you might begin to weave into your day, grounded in ancient wisdom, but deeply needed now:

1. Let Silence Be the First Voice

Before you speak, pause.
Even for just a breath.
Ask inwardly: *Is this necessary? Is it kind? Is it rooted in peace?*

2. Speak with Intent, Not Habit

Speak slowly.
Don't fill the space just because it's empty.
Sometimes, the deepest connections come from shared stillness, not shared stories.

3. Choose Sacred Companionship

The early Celtic monks sought spiritual friends—those with whom silence was comfortable and words were wise.
Seek your anam cara—your soul friend—those with whom you can talk of things that truly matter.

4. Watch for the Energy of Your Words

Notice how your body feels after a conversation.
Lighter? Heavier? Scattered? Grounded?
The soul knows what it needs—and what drains it.

5. Let Your Words Bless

Make it your quiet intention that your speech would heal, not harm.
Even in everyday exchanges, let your

words be seeds of peace, not sparks of noise.

A Sacred Reminder

You don't have to explain yourself all the time.
You don't have to keep up the conversation just because everyone else is.
You are not less spiritual because you're quiet.
You are not more spiritual because you talk about spiritual things.

You are becoming more whole each time you choose peace over performance.
More real each time you choose depth over noise.
More true each time you choose silence over surface.

A Blessing for the Tongue and the Soul

May your words be few, but full.
May your silence be strong enough to speak for you.
May your conversations be like wells—
deep, clear, and nourishing.
And when the noise of the world rises,
may your heart remember the sacredness of stillness.

Feeling Scattered? This Might Be Why.

We live in a time where everyone seems to know what everyone else is doing.
We scroll, we compare, we comment. We hear every opinion, every update, every argument.
And yet, many of us can't hear ourselves anymore.
We don't know how to listen inward.
We've forgotten how to be still long enough to meet God.

When Attention Scatters, the Soul Does Too

Most of us are constantly extending ourselves outward—into other people's business, opinions, and choices. We mean well. We want to help, understand, participate. But without even noticing, we begin living more in other people's worlds than in our own.

We give away our attention.
We lose track of our purpose.
We wonder why peace feels so far away.
But peace doesn't live in the noise. It never has.

Celtic Christianity and the Wisdom of Withdrawal

The early Celtic Christians were deeply involved in the world—but they were not consumed by it.
They made time to withdraw to the quiet edges of creation—not as escape, but as alignment.
They understood that the soul needs solitude to grow, just as a seed needs darkness and stillness to take root.

They would walk slowly through fields, pause beside rivers, pray in the stillness of the morning. Not because they were hiding from life—but because they were seeking a deeper way to live it.

The Distraction of Being Over-Involved

It's easy to confuse spiritual activity with spiritual growth.
But true transformation rarely comes from staying busy.
You can read every book.
You can be in all the right circles.
You can say all the right words.
And still feel empty.
Because real growth asks something quieter, something harder. It asks you to be present to your own soul.

The Gentle Work of Interior Recalibration

Instead of chasing spiritual intensity or clinging to your initial burst of inspiration, the invitation is this:
Come back to the core.
It's not about trying harder.
It's about clearing space.

Not to become perfect—but to become *available*.
To grace.
To truth.
To transformation.
And to do that, you'll need to begin noticing what draws you away from yourself.

What Happens When You Tend to the Inner Life

When we stop pouring energy into things that do not feed us, something begins to shift:
Our nervous system settles.
Our spiritual hunger clarifies.
Our sense of identity becomes less fragile.
We move from being reactive to being rooted.
We stop grasping at other people's stories and begin living our own again.

Modern Soul-Tending: Practices for Returning to Peace

If you're longing for spiritual steadiness, try this:

1. Tend to What's Yours

You don't have to carry every story, follow every drama, or weigh in on every issue. You are not responsible for fixing what is not yours.
Focus on your own soul's unfolding.

2. Make Space Daily
Create a rhythm that includes stillness. Turn off the noise. Go for a quiet walk. Sit with the trees.
Let your body remember what peace feels like.

3. Let Growth Be Quiet
Spiritual progress isn't always obvious. Sometimes it looks like not reacting. Sometimes it feels like releasing a habit or thought you've held for too long. Sometimes it's simply remembering you're loved, exactly as you are.

4. Break Habits That Scatter You
Notice where you automatically give away your energy.

What apps, patterns, or people pull you out of your centre?
What could you gently release, even a little?

5. Begin Again—Gently

If you feel further from peace than you used to, don't panic.
You haven't lost anything. You're being invited back.
And you don't need to leap—you just need to turn.
A small return is still a return.

A Whisper for the Soul-Worn

You were not made to live fragmented.
You don't need to chase growth.
You don't need to perform your spirituality.
You don't need to fix everything at once.
You are allowed to quiet your life.
To return to what is slow, real, and deeply

rooted.
To become simple again.
And from that still place, something holy will rise.

A Blessing for the Way Back

May you stop chasing what was never meant to be yours.
May your attention return to your own soul.

May you remember that peace lives not in the noise—but in the still, sacred space within.
And may the slow work of Spirit find you willing—again, and again, and again.

When Love Becomes the Reason

It's easy to mistake busyness for goodness.
We fill our calendars with acts of service, our hands with worthy projects, our conversations with causes and commitments.
We love the feeling of being useful, important, even irreplaceable.

But beneath all our striving, a deeper question waits:

Who are we really doing it for?

The answer to that question changes everything.

When Good Works Become Something Else

There's a way to do all the right things—feed the hungry, encourage the weary, build beautiful things—and yet still be rooted more in ego than in love.

It happens quietly:

- We serve because it makes us feel good about ourselves.
- We give because we want to be noticed—or at least not forgotten.
- We help because it makes the world feel a little more under control.

None of these are evil. They are very human.
But they miss the deeper mark.

In the wisdom of the saints—and echoed across Celtic Christian practice—the worth of a work is not in its scale or its recognition, but in the purity of the love behind it.

Without love, even the grandest actions ring hollow.
With love, even the smallest kindness shimmers with eternal weight.

The Celtic Understanding of True Charity

The early Celtic monks understood that greatness wasn't measured in visible achievements.
It was measured in hidden faithfulness.
It was shaped in obscurity, carved in solitude, and offered freely without clinging to the outcome.

They often spoke of anam cara, the soul friend—not someone who made you feel good, but someone who called you back to your truest self.
In the same way, true charity doesn't always make you feel triumphant.
Sometimes, it humbles you.
It empties you.
It reminds you that every good thing you offer was given to you first.

True charity is less about how much you do—and more about how freely you love.

Love Without Self in the Centre

The world often teaches us to ask, *"What will I get out of this?"*
True charity asks, *"How can God be seen more clearly through this?"*

When love becomes the centre instead of self:

- We stop needing credit for our good deeds.
- We stop comparing our efforts to others'.
- We stop tying our worth to how much we accomplish.

Instead, we begin to measure the day by gentleness, not by productivity.
We look not at what we can grasp, but what we can offer without strings.

This is a quieter kind of success.
But it's the only kind that truly lasts.

The Risk of Doing Good for the Wrong Reasons

It's a sobering truth: Not every good action is born of good intentions.

Some acts of kindness are rooted in self-importance.
Some are tangled up in guilt.
Some spring from a need to be needed.

Even love itself can be used as a way to manipulate, control, or prove something.

This is why the ancient teachers so often warned about hidden motives.
Because even in the realm of charity, the ego loves to build its little kingdoms.

The test is simple but challenging:
Am I willing to love, even if I am unseen, misunderstood, or forgotten?

If the answer is yes—then the love is likely real.

Measuring Success by God's Light, Not the World's

The world measures success in visibility, volume, and applause.
Heaven measures it in hidden faithfulness.

The Celtic saints lived in this tension every day.
They walked windswept paths few others trod.
They built tiny, crumbling oratories.
They healed in silence.
They blessed without expecting thanks.

They trusted that the smallest act of love—offered purely—was more powerful than the most impressive achievement done for show.

What if we believed that again?

When Loving Means Letting Go

Sometimes the most loving thing we can do is to release our plans.
To postpone our "good works" in order to meet someone where they really are.
To pause our striving long enough to notice the actual need in front of us.

Real love is flexible.
Real love listens.
Real love bends and adapts without losing its centre.

Sometimes the holiest thing you can do is change your plans for the sake of someone else's suffering.
Not to abandon your calling—but to let love shape it moment by moment.

What True Charity Looks Like in Everyday Life

It's not always grand gestures.
It's often the almost invisible acts:

- Pausing to truly listen when someone needs to speak.//
- Giving without needing acknowledgment.
- Offering kindness when there's nothing to gain.
- Praying for someone who will never know you did.
- Choosing the quieter way, the slower way, the gentler word.

None of these may ever be recognized. But all of them are seeds planted in the eternal garden of God's heart.

A Different Kind of Legacy

One day, all the titles, achievements, platforms, and polished reputations will pass away.

But what will remain is every unseen act of love.
Every silent prayer.
Every choice to serve without seeking applause.
Every yes to grace when no one was looking.

That is the true work.
That is the real inheritance.

Final Reflection

If you do something beautiful today and no one notices—God notices.
If you love someone well and they never thank you—your soul grows stronger

anyway.
If you give and no one gives back—
something eternal is still being built.

You are not here to be impressive.
You are here to be faithful.
You are here to be love in motion.

In the end, the only work that matters is
the work done in love.

And even the smallest spark of true
charity can outshine the brightest
achievements of a self-seeking heart.

The People Who Test Us May Be the Ones Who Shape Us Most

No one warns you that the deeper you go into the spiritual life, the more uncomfortable you'll feel with your own expectations of others.

It's easy to begin this path imagining that, in time, everyone around you will also grow. That grace will smooth out the rough edges—not just in yourself, but in those closest to you. That patience and understanding will blossom naturally. That your gentleness will be mirrored back to you.

Then life happens. People don't change at your pace. They continue to irritate, to miss the point, to press your buttons. And you find yourself thinking, "Surely by now, they should know better." Or worse, "I should be past being bothered by this."

But the truth is: spiritual maturity doesn't protect you from frustration. What it does—when it's real—is ask you to meet frustration differently.

The Work of Bearing with One Another

One of the most overlooked spiritual practices is this: learning to bear with others.
Not "tolerate." Not "put up with." But genuinely, humbly, bear with.

That's different. Bearing with someone means walking alongside them, even when their patterns rub against yours. It means seeing their imperfections not as threats or failures, but as part of their humanity—and part of your opportunity to grow.

Of course, it's hard. Much harder than silence, or passive-aggression, or cutting someone off and calling it "boundaries." There's a time for boundaries, yes. But far more often, what we really need is the internal capacity to stay open.

And that only happens when we stop assuming people exist to make our lives easier.

When Correction Isn't the Point

We love the idea of others changing. Especially when their faults inconvenience us.

We want people to be more self-aware. More disciplined. More emotionally intelligent. More spiritual. More agreeable. We want them to stop interrupting, stop making a mess of things, stop being so inconsistent, so opinionated, so slow to learn.

But here's the uncomfortable truth: it's far easier to focus on other people's faults than it is to admit our own.

We often believe that our frustration is about their behaviour.
But much of the time, it's actually about our unmet expectations, our desire to feel in control, or our discomfort with unpredictability.

This is why the ancient teachers warned against the illusion of trying to perfect others. It's not just unkind—it's a spiritual distraction.

The Danger of Unequal Measures

There's a strange inconsistency in how we treat faults—our own, and others'.
We want grace for ourselves, and justice for everyone else.
We understand the reasons we act out of fear, tiredness, or pride—but when others do the same, we call it character failure.

It's easy to forget that our frustrations with others often mirror things we haven't yet healed in ourselves.

The ego is clever. It hides behind standards and ideals. It says, "I just want them to be better," when what it often means is, "I want them to be more like me."

But the goal of the spiritual life isn't to make others into our image. It's to allow both ourselves and others to be transformed into something much larger—into love itself.

Celtic Spirituality and the Grace of Imperfection

In Celtic Christianity, the spiritual path was never seen as solitary. Even the hermits who sought solitude often returned to community—because it was in relationship that their inner work was truly tested.

They expected friction.
They expected discomfort.
They expected to be wrong about people sometimes—and to be wrong about themselves.

But they also believed that these imperfections were not obstacles to the divine—they were the very place where God could do the deepest work.

Community, with all its mess, was a sacred furnace. It burned away illusion. It refined motives. And it taught the kind of love that isn't dependent on everything going smoothly.

A Test of Strength and Temper

It's tempting to think that bearing with others is a sign of weakness. That being "soft" means being walked over. But bearing with someone—not enabling, not fixing, but simply walking beside—is one of the strongest things you can do.

It requires emotional discipline.
It requires self-awareness.
It requires trust that transformation is God's work, not ours.

In times of friction, the question is not, "How do I make them change?"

It's, "Who am I becoming as I respond to this?"

Because in the end, adversity doesn't create our temperament—it reveals it.

Some People Will Not Change on Your Schedule

There will be people in your life who do not improve, who do not learn, who do not soften. At least, not when or how you hoped they would.

And that has to be okay.

Your job isn't to hurry their journey or write their story. Your job is to be faithful in yours.

Sometimes, that means giving space.
Sometimes, it means offering grace again.
Sometimes, it means holding sorrow for

what could have been, and letting it be what it is.

What matters is how you show up—not how they respond.

Bearing One Another Is How We Are Remade

The uncomfortable people, the irritating people, the stubborn, loud, unpredictable, defensive, overly sensitive, distant, too-needy people—these are not detours in our path.

They are the path.

Not because we're supposed to fix them, but because in choosing to love anyway, we ourselves are softened. Humbled. Grown.

God did not design community to be convenient. He designed it to be holy.

And holiness, in this case, looks like staying. Bearing. Loving. Trusting. Not because it's easy—but because we are being transformed.

A Life Set Apart: Embracing the Pilgrim's Path in the Everyday

There comes a quiet yearning in the soul. It does not begin with thunder or trumpet blasts, but with a subtle disquiet—a sense that the life we are living, though full, is not yet whole. That beyond the emails and the errands, the appearances and aspirations, there is something more—a deeper rhythm, a clearer path, a truer way of being.

This inner pull is ancient. It echoes through the lives of mystics, monks, and seekers, and it stirs again in the hearts of many today. In the Celtic Christian tradition, it was often framed as a longing for the *anam cara*, the soul-friend, or the *peregrinatio*, the wandering pilgrim who left behind all for the sake of God.

To live a religious life, in this older sense, is not about withdrawing from the world. It is about stepping more consciously into it—with sacred intent and a willing heart. It means choosing a way that is radically countercultural: a life not based on achievement, recognition, or gain, but rooted instead in presence, humility, and devotion.

The Monastery of the Everyday

In this sense, the monastery is no longer confined to stone walls and sacred chants—it becomes the kitchen sink, the traffic jam, the patient listening in a difficult conversation. Every moment can be cloaked in presence. Every act an opportunity to practice faithfulness.

To live as one devoted to God does not require renunciation of the world but requires that we meet the world with open eyes and an open heart. It is not ease we are called to, but embodiment.

This is not the fashionable spirituality of curated retreats or carefully filtered quotes. It is the hidden work. The daily discipline. The long obedience in the same direction. And yet, it is here that the deepest joy is found—because this way of living begins to draw us into alignment with the sacredness that underpins all things.

Becoming Exile, Becoming Pilgrim

The soul who chooses the religious life will inevitably feel like a stranger at times. This is not a flaw, but a signpost.

To walk with a pilgrim's heart is to accept that you may no longer fit easily into the values and rhythms around you. You may be called a fool. You may be misunderstood. You may question your own path more than once. But this dislocation is part of the invitation.

The Celtic monks spoke often of *exile for the love of Christ*—a chosen dislocation that opened them to grace. They would sail without oar or compass, trusting the Spirit to carry them where they were most needed. This wasn't about recklessness. It was about radical trust. About letting go of the need to control every outcome and instead living in surrender to the deeper flow of grace.

Today, exile may not mean sailing to distant shores. It may mean becoming inwardly free from the need to be liked, the craving for applause, the constant temptation to measure our worth by our productivity. It may mean stepping into conversations others avoid. Choosing stillness over noise. Forgiveness over vengeance. Depth over popularity.

And in this chosen exile, we find the pilgrim's joy—not in having arrived, but in walking the road with God.

Letting Go to Grow

In older writings, the spiritual journey was often described as requiring "mortification" of the self. Today, that word carries painful connotations that can be easily misunderstood. But in its original sense, it simply pointed to the need to let go of our attachments—to pride, control, comfort, or ego—in order to be made new.

This is not about punishment or self-denial for its own sake. It's about creating space for what is truer, softer, and more alive in us to come forth. Like a sculptor gently chipping away stone to reveal the form within, the soul's work is to clear what obscures the image of God within.

Letting go to grow means choosing forgiveness over resentment, presence over distraction, humility over defensiveness. It is not a grand performance but a quiet interior shift. A series of small, faithful turnings.

This is the path of transformation. Of becoming more real, more rooted, more radiant.

Humility: The Hidden Jewel

No one who longs for a life of depth can avoid the path of humility. It is not about playing small or hiding your light. It is about showing up truthfully—without the need to inflate or diminish yourself.

To be "least and servant of all" is not about weakness; it is the greatest strength. It is the ability to meet others in love, without needing to prove, perform, or posture.

Humility frees us to be present. To really see the person in front of us. To listen without defence. To love without condition. It is tested most in the context of community—with family, with colleagues, with those we find difficult.

And yet, it is in these relationships that humility can flower into something truly beautiful: compassion, patience, wisdom.

The Celtic saints understood this. They did not live above others, but among them. As healers, teachers, and companions. Their holiness was not marked by separation, but by service.

So it is for us. We are not called to shine in isolation, but to illuminate the path for others as we walk together.

Fool for Love

To live this way will not always make sense to others. You may be misunderstood. You may be told you're too idealistic, too sensitive, too much.

Let it be so.

This is the way of the holy fool—the one who chooses love over cynicism, gentleness over sarcasm, integrity over image. Not because it's easy, but because it's true.

The world may not reward this path. But the soul will.

You may not win the argument, but you will keep your peace. You may not get the last word, but you will find your centre. You may not be praised, but you will be free.

And in that freedom, you will become a quiet revolution—an invitation for others to remember what really matters.

Refined by Grace

The spiritual life is not tidy. It is not always calm. There are moments of deep wrestling, of dry seasons, of aching questions. But even these are part of the refinement.

The ancient image is gold in the furnace. Not destroyed, but purified. Not burnt up, but made radiant.

You will not be the same person you were when you began. And that is grace.

Not the grace of ease, but of depth. Not the grace of answers, but of presence. Not the grace of having it all together, but of being wholly, wildly loved as you are.

The Hidden Wholeness

To live a life set apart is not to run from the world but to meet it differently. To see the sacred shimmering beneath the surface. To carry the presence of God not as a banner, but as a breath.

This life does not require perfection. It asks only this: be faithful. Be present. Be real.

And in doing so, you will walk the path of the ancient ones. The pilgrims. The monks. The mothers and fathers of faith. And you will discover that the way of devotion is not far off—it is here, now, waiting to be lived.

So step into the sacred ordinary. Carry the fire of love. And walk on.

The Gift of Withdrawal: On the Love of Solitude and Silence

There is a kind of peace that cannot be found in noise.

Not because the world is evil or broken beyond repair, but because the soul was not made to be endlessly scattered. There is something within us—deep and old and holy—that longs to return to stillness. To step out of the current. To sit, to breathe, and to listen.

In Celtic lands, the saints knew this well. They sought not fame, nor comfort, but solitude. Not as an escape from life, but as a way of deepening into it. Saint Cuthbert withdrew to the Farne Islands, content with wind and birds for company. Saint Kevin made his home in a narrow cave beside a lake. Even Brigid, who carried the fire of community in her heart, would retreat to silence for renewal. These were not acts of avoidance. They were expressions of love.

To love solitude is not to hate the world. It is to trust that God waits in the quiet.

We are surrounded today by voices. Notifications. Headlines. Performances. Expectations. It is easier than ever to fill every moment with noise, and harder than ever to hear our own hearts. That is why we must make space. Solitude is not a luxury for the few. It is a necessity for the soul.

There is a room within each of us—a sacred inner chamber—where the noise of the world cannot reach. But we must choose to enter it. We must, as the Psalm says, *commune with our own heart and be still.* This is not a call to isolation. It is a call to intimacy. To come apart with God. To dwell in the company of the Holy One.

In silence, we see our distractions for what they are. In silence, the soul sheds its masks. In silence, the deep questions begin to rise. In silence, God speaks—not in thunder, but in stillness.

And what is revealed is not always comfortable. Silence can show us our pride, our compulsions, our fear of being unimportant. But if we stay, if we wait, if we listen, we begin to hear another voice—not of shame, but of love. The voice that calls us by name.

The saints often warned of "idle goings about" and "trifling conversations." Not because conversation is bad—but because words carry weight. The more we speak without reflection, the more our hearts grow dull. It is easier, as they said, to remain silent than to speak wisely. Easier to stay home than to guard your soul in the crowd.

The practice of solitude is not withdrawal in the negative sense—not a retreat from responsibility or love. Rather, it is withdrawal in order to return differently. To come back not with more to say, but with more to give.

We fast from noise so we can be more present. We unplug so we can reconnect. We hide, not to disappear, but to become more fully ourselves. This is the paradox of sacred withdrawal: that in stepping back, we return closer to the heart of things.

There is a sweetness to the quiet heart. But it does not come quickly. We must stay with the silence long enough to be shaped by it.

Holy compunction—that tender sorrow that opens the heart—comes not in the rush, but in the stillness. Tears rise not in performance, but in presence. And from those tears flows healing. Reconnection. Grace.

This is not self-pity, nor guilt. It is a return to softness. To the knowledge that we need God, and that God delights in meeting us in our need. Those who practice this often find the Scriptures come alive again. That prayer becomes less a task and more a breath. That peace returns. Not because the world has changed. But because they have.

We are all tempted by novelty. Drawn toward entertainment, toward gossip, toward "just one more thing." But how often do we return from such wanderings weary? How often do we pay for distraction with a restless heart?

We seek amusement, but come home empty. We seek connection, but end up more scattered.

Solitude teaches us to hunger for what truly satisfies. It reminds us that we don't need to see or know everything. That the heavens and the earth—the grasses, the trees, the stones—are already enough to evoke awe.

What can we see abroad that we cannot see in the quiet gaze of God?

Let this be the gentle call: not to flee life, but to embrace it more deeply. Not to fear the world, but to no longer be owned by it.

Close the door. Still the noise. Sit down.

Let Jesus find you there.

Let your solitude become sanctuary. Let your silence become song. Let your chamber become the thin place where heaven brushes earth.

And when you go out again, you will carry the quiet with you. Not as escape. But as light.

Tears That Heal: A Journey Into Soulful Sorrow and Joy

There is a sorrow that does not crush but opens.

It is not the sorrow of despair, nor the heaviness of shame. It is a holy sorrow—a compunction of heart—that softens what has grown hard within us and invites us to kneel before the truth of things with tears not of guilt, but of grace.

To feel compunction is to become human again.

Rediscovering Holy Sorrow

In our culture, we are taught to numb and distract. Pain is a problem to be solved, sorrow an inconvenience to be silenced. But the ancient saints knew better. They taught that tears can be sacred. That grief can be a doorway. That compunction is not a punishment, but a gift.

Compunction is the soul's ache for God. It arises not from perfection, but from the awareness of our imperfection, held in the light of mercy. It is not neurotic guilt or obsessive regret—it is a yearning to be whole, a recognition of the gap between who we are and who we are becoming.

The Saints and Their Tears

This sacred sorrow clears space within us. It softens pride. It burns away distraction. It makes room for God.

Saint Columba, it is said, wept often over his youthful arrogance and the conflicts it caused. And yet it was through those tears that his heart was softened, and he became a source of healing for others. Likewise, Saint Brendan, known for his voyage, sought silence and prayer not to escape the world, but to deepen his heart's response to it.

To walk with compunction is to walk with awareness. Not anxiety. But honest, humble attentiveness to the condition of the soul.

Leaving the Lesser Joys

The ancient texts warn us not to seek too much freedom. Not because freedom is bad, but because unguarded liberty can scatter the heart. A soul stretched too thin cannot rest in God.

Much of what we call joy is often distraction in disguise. It tickles but does not satisfy. It entertains but does not nourish. Compunction teaches us to long for something deeper. A joy that does not flee in silence. A peace that does not fade in solitude.

This is why the saints turned from worldly mirth. Not because they despised life, but because they desired it whole.

A Holy Discomfort

We rarely change while we are comfortable. Compunction stirs us. It unsettles the soul just enough to wake it.

To feel the weight of our shortcomings is not to be condemned by them. It is to stand in truth. A truth that brings us to tears not because we are unloved, but because we are loved too deeply to be left unchanged.

A heart that has known compunction begins to see differently. It no longer seeks escape, but redemption. It does not cling to distraction, but finds peace in the Presence that remains.

The Gift of Tears

There is a poverty of spirit that complains constantly. But there is also a poverty of spirit that opens the floodgates of prayer.

The ancient Celtic monks often prayed for the gift of tears. Not dramatic weeping, but a steady stream of soul-softening grace. They saw tears as healing water, as signs that the heart was alive again.

We might do well to pray for the same. Not to dwell in sorrow, but to let sorrow do its work—to clean the lens of the soul.

If we wept more over the true things—the ache of separation from God, the brokenness of the world, the places we've grown cold—we might find that joy returns with more depth, more tenderness.

Keeping the Heart Awake

Compunction teaches us to keep watch. It reminds us that we are not yet whole. That there are places in us still waiting to be healed, transformed, redeemed.

We live in a time that treats seriousness as a flaw. Everything must be light, amusing, immediate. But a spiritual life that only dances and never weeps is incomplete.

We are pilgrims. And pilgrims walk with tears in their eyes, not because they are hopeless, but because they are going home.

The fear of God is not terror, but reverent awareness. The soul who walks in that awareness lives with a kind of gravity— not heaviness, but depth.

And that depth is the soil in which real joy grows.

To Weep with Jesus

The call to compunction is not a call to morbid introspection. It is a call to intimacy. Jesus Himself wept. Over cities. Over death. Over love withheld.

To weep with Jesus is to walk close beside Him.

It is to feel what He feels. To love what He loves. To ache where He aches.

It is the heart's response to divine beauty meeting human frailty.

And in that sacred meeting, something shifts. The soul becomes more pliable. The conscience more tender. The will more surrendered.

Tears become a prayer, and sorrow becomes a path.

The Last Word Is Love

Compunction is not the end. It is the beginning of transformation. It breaks the shell of the hardened heart so that grace can enter.

If you feel far from God, ask for tears. If your heart has grown cold, sit in

stillness and ask to feel again.
If joy feels shallow, let sorrow deepen it.

The one who learns to weep in the arms of God finds a joy the world cannot steal.

And in the silence after the tears, Love speaks.

Not to shame, but to call.
Not to condemn, but to restore.
Not to wound, but to welcome.

This is the grace of compunction: not sorrow that ends in despair, but sorrow that ends in union.

The way home is wet with tears. But it leads to joy.

The Ache You Can't Name: How to Find Meaning When Life Feels Hard

There is a truth we often resist: that life, as we know it here, is laced with suffering. No matter how carefully we build it, how earnestly we seek pleasure, security, or ease—something always escapes us. Rest is fleeting. Joy, though real, is often tempered. The ache of the world is not an anomaly. It is part of our condition.

And yet, to contemplate this misery is not an act of despair. It is an invitation to turn, not to the world for relief, but to God for meaning.

The Universal Ache

Why are we so often disquieted when life doesn't unfold according to our desires?

Who among us has not asked this in some form? We strive for happiness, but it slips through our fingers. We watch others and imagine they have it easier, more sorted, more fulfilled. Yet all of us—rich and poor, spiritual or worldly—carry the weight of life.

The one who is strongest is not the one who avoids suffering but the one who is strong enough to suffer something for love's sake, for meaning, for God.

That shift—from resistance to purpose—is the beginning of inner strength.

The Great Illusion

There is a kind of madness in how we chase after temporal things, as if they might finally make us whole. "See how prosperous he is," we say. "See how much she has." But everything that glitters fades. Everything visible is temporary.

Those who walk the ancient paths knew this well. The Celtic saints were no strangers to hardship. They lived in windswept cells, walked barefoot across rocky terrain, and let go of comfort for the sake of clarity.

Not because they were stoics. But because they had seen the deeper beauty.

Saint Cuthbert lived among the sea birds and seals. Saint Ita taught children to love holiness over praise. They longed not for wealth or ease, but for hearts unburdened by the weight of illusion.

To long for God is to grow disenchanted with the world's false promises.

A Bittersweet Life

The more spiritually awake we become, the more we feel the ache of life. The body's needs, the pull of temptation, the fragmentation of our attention—all feel like burdens once we've tasted something more.

Even eating, sleeping, and working can feel heavy to the devout soul who longs for purity and union. This is not to hate the world, but to recognise its limits. The spiritual person doesn't disdain life; they simply don't idolise it.

The ache becomes a compass.

The Blindness of Contentment

There are those who live chained to the fleeting. Even when it offers no peace, they cling to it—choosing distraction over depth. They would rather live in noise than face the silence. Rather labour endlessly than ask what it's for.

The saints, on the other hand, let go. They did not despise the earth, but they held it lightly. Their hearts leaned upward.

They lived with an awareness that we often try to drown out: that this life is not home.

The Invitation to Begin Again

If you feel weighed down, uncertain, or dull in spirit, hear this: there is still time. The path has not closed. The hour has not passed.

Now is the time to act. Now is the moment to begin.

True growth rarely comes when we are comfortable. It comes when we are agitated. When we are frustrated. When we are weary enough to seek a deeper rest.

It is through fire and water, says the psalm, that God brings us into a spacious place. We do not reach freedom by coasting, but by pressing forward—even through discomfort.

The Struggle Within

It is humbling how quickly we fall. How easily we forget our resolutions. How often we promise to change, only to find ourselves back where we began.

This, too, is part of the path.

We are frail. We are forgetful. We are unstable. But we are not without hope. The call is not to perfection, but to perseverance.

The more we see our weakness, the more we are invited into grace. Not as a concept, but as a lifeline.

A New Beginning

It is not too late to grow. Even if we feel like novices. Even if we have wandered far. Even if our fire has burned low.

Begin again.

Not tomorrow. Now.

Say yes to the next right thing.

Die Before You Die: The Sacred Invitation of Mortality

What if the most urgent spiritual teaching isn't hidden in ancient books or shouted from pulpits—but whispered softly by death?

Not in fear. But in invitation.

To meditate on death is not to become morbid, but to become fully alive. To strip away illusion. To see clearly. And perhaps, to begin at last to live as we were always meant to.

Facing the Vanishing Point

One moment we are here. The next, we are not. One breath, one heartbeat—then silence. This is not a threat, but a truth. The fragile impermanence of life is not something to be ignored or feared, but embraced as part of the sacred fabric of our being.

Still, we forget. We distract. We act as though we are owed a long life, as though tomorrow is a guarantee. We plan, we delay, we say, "Someday I'll change. Someday I'll go deeper."

But someday is not promised.

To live in light of death is to be awake to life. It is to ask, today: *What truly matters? What am I carrying that no longer serves? If this were my last sunrise, would I meet it in peace?*

The Soul's Sobering Companion

When we meditate on our mortality, we're not rehearsing dread—we're remembering truth.

It is sobering to realise how quickly we are forgotten. Even those who love us will move on, as they must. We are but a shadow, passing briefly across the earth. But this awareness doesn't have to lead to despair. It can lead to freedom.

Freedom from striving. From proving. From hoarding time, love, or forgiveness.

The saints and mystics knew this. They did not deny death—they befriended it. They walked as pilgrims, as strangers in a land not their own. They wore the world lightly and lived with a heart always leaning homeward.

The Call to Begin Now

We postpone our souls. We wait until we're more settled, more holy, more ready. But death is not impressed by our procrastination. It moves at its own pace. And often, it comes quietly.

So the invitation is simple: *Begin now*.

Now is the moment to forgive. To pray. To speak truth. To walk barefoot through the holy spaces of your own life.

Now is the day of salvation.

Now is the time to awaken.

If you've delayed what matters most, don't waste time mourning the delay. Start again. Begin where you are.

A Holy Unknowing

Every illness, every loss, every encounter with fragility is a teacher. Death does not knock politely. It breaks in. It reshapes the room. And sometimes, it is through this intrusion that the deepest clarity comes.

How many have been taken in a moment—by accident, illness, tragedy? And how many of us, even knowing this, still live as though we are immortal?

To live in readiness is not to live in fear. It is to live with courage. It is to befriend each hour as a gift, to release each moment with grace.

What Will Remain?

At the end, what will matter?

Not the status. Not the possessions. Not the number of years, but the quality of presence.

Have we loved well?
Have we lived honestly?
Have we forgiven freely?

Have we trusted in the mercy that holds us beyond breath?

These are the treasures that endure.

Living as One Who Is Dying

Strangely, the people most at peace are often those who have faced death and surrendered to it. The Celtic monks spoke of the daily dying—of dying before you die—so that when the final hour comes, it finds you already in the rhythm of release.

To die daily is to detach with gentleness. To let go of ego, of envy, of every unnecessary burden. To live each day in a way that would make your final breath a holy one.

This is not resignation. It is resurrection in disguise.

A Soul Turned Homeward

In the end, we are all walking each other home. The best preparation for death is to live with eternity in mind. To walk lightly. To pray deeply. To love without reserve.

Keep your heart free. Keep your soul awake. Make friends with the silence. Learn to speak with God in the dark.

And let your life become what your death will reveal it to be: not an ending, but a becoming.

What If Your Struggles Are Actually Saving You?

There are seasons in life that feel like being stretched thin across too many pressures. You're doing your best, maybe even doing good things, and still—something comes along to contradict your efforts, to trip up your intentions. Maybe it's a harsh word. A misunderstanding. A loss you didn't see coming.

It's tempting to see these moments as interruptions or setbacks. But what if they're something more? What if adversity isn't a failure or punishment—but part of the path itself?

For centuries, the saints and mystics—including the early Celtic Christians—viewed hardship not as a detour but as a kind of refining fire. They understood that the uncomfortable moments, the unchosen struggles, often have a strange way of bringing us back to the only place where true peace is found: God.

Letting Go of the Illusion of Control

We live in a world that praises certainty, strength, and forward motion. But adversity has a way of unravelling all three. It pulls us into uncomfortable uncertainty. It exposes where we've placed our trust. And it slows us down whether we want it to or not.

Yet in this very undoing, something important is revealed: how much we've been relying on things that cannot ultimately hold us. Reputation. Comfort. The good opinion of others. A plan that goes exactly the way we imagined.

Adversity removes the illusion of control. And while that might feel like a loss at first, it's actually a doorway into something much more solid.

The Celtic Path of Holy Resilience

In the Celtic Christian tradition, there's a strong theme of learning through the land, the seasons, and the struggles. Life wasn't expected to be easy. The saints didn't pray for things to always go well—they prayed for strength, for humility, and for the presence of God in all things.

Stories of figures like St. Cuthbert or St. Brigid often highlight their response to adversity as a holy encounter. When storms came—literally or metaphorically—they didn't assume they'd done something wrong. Instead, they looked for what was being refined in them. They accepted that part of the spiritual journey would be hardship, contradiction, and even being misunderstood.

They let adversity do its deep work, which was often the work of humbling, purifying, and re-centring.

Modern Struggles, Ancient Answers

Today, when things go wrong, we tend to look outward for answers. We try to solve the problem, distract ourselves, or look for someone to blame. The discomfort of being judged unfairly or having life go against us can quickly trigger anxiety, frustration, or self-doubt.

But if we allow ourselves to pause, to step back and ask what this difficulty might be offering—not just what it's taking away—we can begin to see adversity as an invitation.

Difficulties have a way of stripping us back to the essentials. They remind us of our dependence on something greater. They make us ask deeper questions: Who am I when things don't go according to plan? Where is my identity rooted? What am I really trusting in?

Adversity often becomes the catalyst for re-aligning our lives with what truly matters.

The Quiet Shift That Changes Everything

One of the most important things adversity teaches is that we're not meant to find perfect peace in this world. As comforting as that sounds, it's also liberating. It reminds us that our hope was never supposed to rest in the success of our plans or the approval of others.

Peace comes not from everything going right, but from being anchored in something deeper. Something unshakeable.

When life presses in and outer support falls away, we're often led to discover the presence of God in a more intimate, unfiltered way. Adversity exposes what is temporary so that we can find what is eternal.

Responding Well: A Few Anchors for Hard Seasons

If you find yourself in a difficult season right now—whether that's external conflict, internal heaviness, or a sense of being misunderstood—here are a few reflections to steady you:

- **You don't need to be seen to be held.** Let go of needing others to understand your motives. Let the peace of being seen by God be enough.

- **Your weariness is not a failure.** When you're tired, it doesn't mean you're doing it wrong. It may mean you're right where the work is happening.

- **You don't need to escape discomfort immediately.** Let the hard season show you what's shifting inside you. It might be making space for something new.

- **Adversity can become alignment.** Use these moments to

ask where you've placed your trust, and gently return it to God.

Final Thoughts

The idea that suffering refines the soul isn't always welcome in today's culture. We're told to fix pain fast, to find silver linings, to move on. But the Celtic saints and mystics remind us that sometimes, peace comes not through avoidance—but through surrender.

Not a giving up, but a letting go—of our grip on outcomes, our need to be right, our longing for ease. In that release, we find something far more steady: the quiet, unwavering presence of God walking with us in the very midst of the hard.

Temptation Isn't the Problem-Avoiding It Is

There's something no one tells you when you begin a spiritual journey:
You don't become immune to struggle—
you become *more aware of it*.

The moment you decide to walk with intention, to orient your life toward God, to live more awake, something stirs. The shadows don't go away. They move in closer. Not to destroy you—but to ask, *"Do you really mean this?"*

We often think of temptation as a singular, dramatic event. But it rarely looks like that. Temptation is often subtle, patient, persistent. It begins as a whisper.

It offers relief, comfort, escape. It doesn't always shout—it waits.

And it always finds us, because it already lives within us.

Why Temptation Is Not a Sign of Failure

In many spiritual traditions, temptation is viewed as a kind of failure or weakness. Something shameful. Something to be hidden. But the older wisdom—the wisdom we find in the desert fathers, the Celtic saints, and the deeper stream of Christian mysticism—tells a different story.

Temptation isn't something that happens *to* you. It's something that reveals *what's already there*. It shows you your attachments, your compulsions, your woundedness, your ego, your pride.

It uncovers the places where your life is still misaligned with your soul.

It's diagnostic, not destructive. Unless you refuse to listen.

In the old monastic path, temptation wasn't a spiritual detour—it was the very arena in which the soul was tested, shaped, and made strong.

The Celtic Way: Struggle as Sacred

The Celtic monks who wandered the coasts and islands of Britain and Ireland didn't do so because they were running from temptation. They did so because they knew that even in the most remote hermitage, temptation would follow. Not just in the form of distractions, but in thoughts, in memories, in desires, in the habits of the flesh.

And so they made peace with the battle.

They learned that temptation was not the enemy. Pride was.
Pretending it wasn't happening was.
Believing they were beyond it was.

So they chose the path of humility, of honesty, of continual prayer.
They didn't expect to win every battle.
They expected to be tested.
But they also expected grace to meet them in it.

Temptation Is Not Just About Morality

We've often reduced temptation to a set of moral rules: don't lie, don't cheat, don't lust, don't take more than your share. But at a deeper level, temptation is anything that pulls us away from the present moment, from our true self, and from God.

- It's the temptation to numb when things get uncomfortable.
- The temptation to compare when we feel insecure.
- The temptation to control when life feels chaotic.
- The temptation to isolate when we feel ashamed.
- The temptation to grasp at power, attention, or success when we feel unseen.

Temptation isn't always dramatic. Sometimes it's as simple as reaching for our phone for the hundredth time today instead of pausing to breathe. Sometimes it's an unspoken jealousy. A silent resentment. A distraction that becomes a way of life.

And often, we don't even realise we've given in until we feel the weight of disconnection settle in.

Why Fighting Isn't Always the Answer

Modern self-help culture tells us to resist temptation by willpower. Fight harder. Be stronger. Think positively. But spiritual wisdom suggests something more enduring: resistance through surrender.

We do not overcome temptation by sheer force of will. We overcome it by humility, honesty, and practice.

We learn to resist not by pushing back harder, but by softening into the presence of God.
By noticing the moment temptation arises.
By admitting what's happening without shame.

By choosing, again and again, to remain aligned with what's real.

We fail, yes. But each time we return, something shifts. The grip loosens. The ego shrinks. The soul grows.

The Anatomy of a Temptation

Most temptations follow the same path:

1. **A subtle suggestion** – a thought, a feeling, a scenario that floats into your awareness.

2. **A growing desire or fear** – you start to imagine what giving in would feel like.

3. **Emotional justification** – you begin to rationalize. "I deserve this." "What's the harm?" "It's just once."

4. **A decision** – conscious or unconscious, you follow the impulse.

5. **The aftermath** – sometimes guilt, sometimes emptiness, sometimes numbness.

The Celtic way was to cut this off early. Not with shame, but with awareness. They knew that if you open the door even a little, the whole storm might enter. So they trained the heart to be watchful, to meet the temptation at the gate.

That watchfulness is not paranoia—it's presence.

Not All Battles Are Equal

Some temptations fade with time. Others revisit you like old ghosts.

Some arise at the beginning of your spiritual path, testing your resolve. Others arrive later, more subtle and refined, testing your integrity.

And some—no matter how far you've come—linger quietly in the background, waiting for a moment of weakness.

There's no shame in being tempted. There's only danger in pretending you're not.

Lessons from the Long Struggle

Here are some soul-wisdoms drawn from the heart of this struggle—lessons the saints lived and that we're invited to rediscover:

- **Temptation is not a sin.** Entertaining it without resistance might be. But the initial stirring is not failure—it's an invitation to awareness.

- **Some battles last a lifetime.** Not because you're failing, but because the shaping of your soul takes time. And some fires burn longer to forge deeper steel.

- **Avoid pride in your victories.** If you resist one temptation today, be grateful—but be humble. Tomorrow may bring a different test.

- **Don't judge others in their battle.** You don't know what war they're fighting. Offer compassion, not condemnation.

- **Temptation reveals what you trust.** Do you rely on your own strength? Or do you let grace carry you through?

Practices for When You're in the Thick of It

1. **Pause and Name It**

    The moment you feel tempted, pause. Name what's happening. "I'm being pulled toward comfort." "This is fear talking." Naming is the first disarming.

2. **Shift Gently**

    Don't shout it down—redirect. Breathe. Walk. Pray. Ask God to come into it with you. Invite grace into the very place that's hurting.

3. **Return to Stillness**

    The heart becomes more vulnerable to temptation when it's tired, distracted, or emotionally overloaded. Build regular stillness into your day. Let your nervous system come home.

4. **Talk to Someone You Trust**
Temptation thrives in silence and shame. Speak it aloud to a trusted friend, spiritual director, or elder. Light weakens its grip.

5. **Know Your Patterns**
Are there times of day, emotional states, or settings where temptation arises most? Prepare for them. Don't be surprised by your humanity.

6. **Anchor Your Identity**
You are not your impulses. You are not your worst thought. You are beloved. You are already home. Temptation doesn't change that.

Temptation as a Path of Transformation

What if we stopped seeing temptation as a shameful enemy, and started seeing it

as a sacred mirror?
A mirror that shows us where we still grasp, still ache, still need healing.

It is not in the absence of struggle that we grow—it is in how we respond to it.
And some of our deepest spiritual growth happens not when we are floating on a cloud of peace, but when we are knee-deep in a battle we didn't choose.

Each time we return, each time we choose the deeper path, the quieter voice, the stillness instead of the shortcut—we become more real. More grounded. More alive in God.

A Final Word for the Weary

If you are tired of struggling—know this:
You are not alone.
You are not broken.
You are being forged.

You are not defined by your temptation.
You are shaped by your return.

And you never return alone.

The Habit That's Quietly Ruining Your Peace (And How to Stop)

There's a certain ease in pointing out what's wrong in other people.
A comfort in naming their faults, questioning their motives, or rolling our eyes at their contradictions. It can even feel... righteous.
But if we're honest, judgment is often a disguise—an emotional shortcut that protects us from looking deeper at ourselves.

And yet, every time we fixate on someone else's flaws, we're quietly being pulled away from the only work that actually transforms us: the work of the heart.

The Reflex to Judge

We all do it.

We hear a snippet of conversation, observe a glance, read a social media post—and before we've even paused to breathe, a story has formed in our mind. A judgment. A conclusion.

We assume intentions.
We label behaviour.
We feel a flicker of superiority, or frustration, or distance.

This all happens in the space of seconds. But it sets the tone for how we relate to the world—and how we lose touch with the sacred ground of compassion.

The problem isn't just that we're being unfair. The deeper issue is that we're missing the chance to become more whole.

The Celtic Wisdom of Seeing Clearly

In the Celtic Christian tradition, judgment wasn't seen as simply a moral failure. It was viewed as a distortion of vision—a fog on the mirror of the soul. To judge others too quickly was to lose sight of God in them—and in ourselves.

Many of the Celtic saints, like St. Brigid and St. Aidan, practiced a kind of holy patience. They understood that every person they met was in process, and that the outer behaviour of someone— especially in moments of stress—rarely revealed the full story of their heart.

To judge too quickly was to assume the role of God.
And to do that was to lose the humility that is the soil of wisdom.

Why We Judge (And Why It Feels Good)

Most of us don't set out to be harsh or unkind. But judgment is seductive. It makes us feel secure. It reinforces our sense of being "right." It helps us momentarily avoid our own discomfort.

But there's more going on under the surface:

- **Projection** – We judge in others what we haven't yet accepted in ourselves.

- **Comparison** – We lift ourselves by lowering others.

- **Fear** – We feel safer when we can neatly categorize people.

- **Control** – If we can label someone, we don't have to sit with the discomfort of not understanding them.

In truth, judging is a way of creating distance.
And the spiritual journey is about closing that distance—with others, with God, and with ourselves.

The Slow Art of Self-Examination

It's easier to scrutinise the faults of others than to sit quietly with the chaos within.

But real transformation begins when we shift our gaze inward—not with shame, but with sacred curiosity.

- What am I really reacting to in this person?
- What part of me feels threatened or insecure?
- What might I be avoiding by focusing on them?
- Is it possible I'm seeing them through the lens of my own unhealed story?

These aren't accusations. They're invitations.

The saints didn't spend their time diagnosing others. They spent their lives asking for clearer vision, deeper wisdom, and the grace to love beyond their own instinct.

The Danger of "Holy" Judgment

One of the subtlest temptations in spiritual life is using holiness as a weapon.

We start to believe our insights, our theology, or our practice gives us a kind of authority to "discern" others. We may call it concern. We may call it truth-telling. But often, it's just judgment in a spiritual costume.

Genuine spiritual maturity is not proven by how clearly you see the flaws in others. It's revealed in how gently you hold them.

What the Mirror Teaches Us

The more time we spend judging others, the less time we spend noticing the movements of our own soul.

And yet, every irritation can be a mirror.
Every reaction, a teacher.
Every misunderstanding, a nudge to grow deeper roots in love.

This doesn't mean we ignore harmful behaviour or never speak truth. But it means we do so with the awareness that we, too, are growing. We, too, are being refined.

It means we speak from a place of empathy, not ego.
From a desire to connect, not to condemn.

Learning to See Differently: A Spiritual Practice

If you feel the impulse to judge someone this week—pause. Take a breath. Then try this:

1. **Ask what story you're telling yourself.** What assumptions are you making? What do you not know?

2. **Consider what the moment might be asking of *you*.** Is there something in this interaction that's inviting you to grow?

3. **Pray for the person.** Even if just for 10 seconds. Bless them. Ask for grace for them. Even that small act can shift everything inside you.

4. **Return your focus inward.** How's your own soul? What's going on in your interior life? What healing might be needed?

You Are Not God. And That's a Good Thing.

There's freedom in letting go of the need to figure everyone out.
There's peace in no longer having to hold the world in judgment.
There's healing in turning your attention inward—not as avoidance, but as sacred tending.

When we focus on understanding rather than judging, something opens.
The soul softens. The presence of God becomes more tangible.
And we begin to see with new eyes—not only others, but ourselves.

Final Reflection

Every time we choose curiosity over criticism, humility over assumption, and silence over certainty, we're walking a deeper path.

A path where the Spirit can move.
A path where love has room to breathe.
A path where we are no longer fixated on controlling others—but free to keep becoming ourselves.

The Flame That Once Burned Bright: Reawakening the Devotion of the Holy Ones

There's something stirring when we read of those who went before us—those luminous souls who gave everything for love. They walked with dust on their feet and fire in their hearts. They fasted, prayed, wept, rejoiced, and surrendered their lives not to applause, but to God. And in doing so, they lit a trail through time.

We call them saints. But they were not born radiant.

They became radiant by choosing the narrow path, over and over again.

Today, when ease is sold as the highest good, the devotion of these holy ones can feel impossibly distant. Yet their lives are not there to shame us—but to awaken something within us. A deeper hunger. A forgotten fire. A quiet invitation to remember who we are, and who we are becoming.

Echoes from the Desert

Long before spiritual retreats and silent getaways became fashionable, there were those who sought solitude not as luxury, but as necessity.

The Desert Fathers and Mothers withdrew to the harsh wilderness of Egypt and Syria—not to escape the world, but to encounter God more fully. Every grain of sand, every harsh wind, became a teacher. They were tempted, tried, and at times tormented—but they held fast, knowing that transformation is often forged in silence.

Closer to home, in the windswept wilds of early Britain and Ireland, Celtic saints answered that same call. They, too, left behind comfort and convention—not to reject the world, but to stand apart from its illusions.

Saint Cuthbert, walking barefoot through frozen streams to pray in the night tide.

Saint Kevin, arms outstretched for hours in devotion, birds nesting in his hands.

Saint Brigid, pouring out her food to feed others, seeing Christ in every stranger.

Saint Aidan, walking from village to village, teaching not with force, but with gentleness and grace.

These weren't perfect people. They were pilgrims. Lovers of God. And their devotion lit up the land.

A Life Poured Out

What marked these holy ones wasn't grandeur. It was the simplicity of lives fully given.

They lived as strangers to the world and yet were intimately bound to it in love. They laboured by day and prayed by night. They gave without counting the cost. They did not seek recognition, and most would be forgotten by name—but their legacy lives on in spirit.

And what strikes us most is not their success but their sincerity. Their capacity to stay faithful in obscurity. Their willingness to be shaped by the slow, steady work of grace.

They were not afraid of hardship. Hunger, cold, rejection, ridicule—none of these stopped them. Because they had found the pearl of great price, and no discomfort could outweigh the joy of communion with God.

And yet... their fire now seems rare.

The Cooling of the Flame

We live in a time where the bar for holiness has been lowered to the ground. If we can simply avoid doing harm, we count ourselves doing well. Endurance has become a virtue merely for surviving the week.

We are not bad people.

But we are often distracted. Fragmented. Pulled in a thousand directions.

The love that once blazed in the hearts of saints has grown lukewarm in the hearts of many—not out of malice, but out of spiritual fatigue.

And yet, we are not without hope.

The ancient flame may flicker, but it is never extinguished. Within each of us is a coal, glowing quietly beneath the ashes, waiting for the breath of the Spirit.

The saints are not meant to be distant icons. They are companions, mentors, and mirrors. Their stories are not trophies, but torches—handed down so we might carry the fire anew.

Rekindling the Way

We do not need to walk into the desert to live with devotion. But we do need to remember how to be still.

We do not need to fast for forty days. But we do need to hunger for the things that truly satisfy.

We do not need to give away everything. But we do need to loosen our grip on what owns us.

We need to remember the practices that open us: prayer that flows from the heart, fasting that unhooks us from illusion, service that expects nothing in return, silence that makes room for the sacred, and community that shapes us in love.

These are not heroic gestures. They are daily choices. Quiet. Hidden. Often unnoticed. But it is precisely here that transformation takes root.

Friends of God

What made the saints radiant was not their discipline alone, but their love. Their deep, aching love for God. A love that gave shape to every action, a love that called them beyond themselves, a love that made them both otherworldly and deeply human.

They were strangers to the world. But to God—they were kin.

Their lives invite us not to imitate their hardship, but to emulate their wholeheartedness.

You don't need to become a monk or mystic. You only need to say yes to the next faithful step. To begin, or begin again. To clear a little space in your day for grace to find you. To choose silence when the world screams noise. To act with courage when your heart longs to retreat. To serve when no one is watching.

You are not alone.

They walked before you. You walk with them now. And others will walk because you dared to.

The Living Thread

There is a thread that runs through the saints, the martyrs, the monastics, the mystics. It is the thread of love made visible. Of faith turned into flesh. Of ordinary lives lived with extraordinary intention.

In Celtic lands, the stories were not written in dusty books but sung into the landscape—told by firelight, carved into stones, whispered by streams and trees. The saints did not seek to be remembered. They sought only to walk closely with God.

And because of that, they became unforgettable.

Their legacy is not just in history, but in you.

If your spirit feels weary, remember theirs. If your hands tremble, let them guide you. If your flame flickers, lean close to their fire.

Let their lives not condemn us—but awaken us. Let them not shame us—but remind us of what is possible.

Even now, the call goes out—not just to admire the saints, but to become one.

Not in perfection, but in pursuit. Not in fame, but in faithfulness. Not in greatness, but in grace.

Living the Inner Vow: A Rhythm of Devotion in the Everyday

To live a life that is both authentic and rooted in the sacred is no small thing. It is to walk a path where your outer life reflects, but never outshines, the inner landscape being quietly shaped by grace. What people see is only ever a shadow of what God sees. And it is the inner life that matters most.

This is not to say appearances don't matter—but rather that the soul is our true altar. The work of a spiritual person is not to perform devotion, but to become devotion. To make of one's life a living vow.

A Daily Beginning

There is wisdom in beginning again. Every single day.

The ancients understood this. In the Celtic Christian tradition, early monks and solitaries like Ita, Columba, and Enda would begin the morning not with a sense of arrival, but with a humble return: *"Lord, help me today to begin again."*

Not with guilt. But with sincerity. Not to strive harder, but to come home to the vow.

This rhythm of daily return—of remembering our heart's intent—is the spine of the spiritual life. We are not called to be perfect. We are called to be present.

Whether through prayer, breath, sacred reading, silence, or simply setting a gentle intention in the morning light, we turn toward the divine and say, *"Let me walk with You today."*

Progress Through Grace

In our culture of self-help and hustle, it is tempting to think our spiritual progress depends on grit alone. But the path of devotion teaches otherwise.

Effort matters. But grace carries.

We resolve, yes. We commit. We build rhythm and rule. But we also acknowledge: all progress is gift. As the proverb says, "Man proposes, but God disposes."

When we fall short—and we will—it is not a sign of failure, but an invitation to trust more deeply. Even our weaknesses, when surrendered, become vessels for transformation. The saints knew this.

They did not glory in their spiritual achievements but returned constantly to humility.

The Sacred Balance

There will be days when prayer is easy, and days when it feels dry. Days when silence is spacious, and days when it is crowded with distraction.

That is why we hold a rhythm.

Morning and evening—two hinges upon which the soul can turn. The dawn for resolution, the dusk for reflection.

How did I walk today? Did I act from love? Did I honour the vow?

This is not self-punishment. It is self-presence. A loving, honest gaze at the life we are shaping.

The inner and outer life mirror each other. The way we tend our tasks, speak to others, move through our work—these are not distractions from our practice. They *are* the practice.

Spiritual Exercises for Ordinary Souls

The phrase "holy exercises" might conjure images of extreme asceticism. But truly, they are just movements of love.

Reading, writing, praying, meditating, serving—all can be sacred. Even walking. Even washing dishes.

In Celtic practice, the sacred was not confined to church walls or holy days. Every act, when done with reverence, became a thin place. Every breath, a chance to commune with the Holy.

And yet, discernment is needed. Not all exercises suit every soul. Not all rhythms fit all seasons. What brings you closer to the heart of God in winter may not sustain you in spring.

Allow yourself permission to adapt. And let your spiritual life breathe.

Secret Devotions, Faithful Duties

There is a deep beauty in secret devotion—those hidden prayers said when no one is watching. But these must never replace our faithfulness to the life we have committed to live outwardly.

Spiritual life is not an escape. It is a commitment. We care for our responsibilities not just out of obligation, but as an extension of our vow. Our duties—to family, to work, to community—are sacred ground.

When space allows, yes, turn inward. Retreat. Reflect. Renew. But let your devotion be integrated, not compartmentalised. Let it flow like a stream through all the terrains of your day.

Seasons of the Soul

There are exercises that suit seasons of joy, and others that hold us through grief. Some that energise in spiritual peace, and others that steady us in temptation.

The liturgical calendar understands this rhythm. In Advent, we wait. In Lent, we strip back. In Easter, we rise. In ordinary time, we walk.

The Celtic saints lived by a natural rhythm of feast and fast, tide and turning. Let your practice reflect this wisdom. Don't force perpetual summer. Let there be seasons.

From one holy day to the next—from Christmas to Candlemas, from Pentecost to All Saints—we live as if preparing to step through the veil. Let every sacred observance be a rehearsal for heaven.

Watching at the Gate

There is no final arrival in this life. We are always in preparation.

But blessed is the one who is found watching. Who keeps the flame lit. Who checks the oil in the lamp. Who lives as if the feast were just beyond the hill.

Not with fear. But with anticipation.

The Celtic way was never about fear of judgment. It was about readiness for joy.

To enter the eternal feast not as stranger, but as beloved.

So let us renew our vows, not as burden, but as delight. Let us begin again each morning, not as those who have failed, but as those who remember.

Let your whole life be your prayer. Let your breath be your yes. Let your days be your vow.

The Sacred Reset: How to Begin Again (and Actually Mean It)

There's something quietly powerful about those moments when we know it's time to change. Not because we've been guilt-tripped into it. Not because someone told us to. But because something deep within says: *It's time.*

Not for a perfect life. But for a more honest one. A more sacred one. A life that finally reflects what matters most.

Remember Why You Started

Somewhere along the line, something stirred you. Maybe it was a breakdown.

Maybe it was beauty. Maybe it was a growing sense that something in the way we live is off—and that life could be deeper, truer, more whole.

That whisper is your soul's compass. And every now and then, it asks you to realign. Not because you're bad. But because you're ready.

Change isn't about fixing what's broken. It's about returning to what's true.

How We Actually Change (Hint: It's Not Overnight)

We all have parts of ourselves that resist growth. Old habits. Old stories. And we all have days where we feel stuck in a loop—like we're always starting over.

But starting over *is* the path. It's the willingness to come back again and again that builds the muscle of transformation. Not dramatic overnight shifts, but small, sacred returns.

Forget the guilt. Forget the pressure to get it right. Just come back.

Show up again.

The Power of Now (Yes, Really)

Someone once asked in prayer, "If only I knew I'd make it in the end, I'd try harder now."

And the quiet answer came: *Then live now as you would then.*

We don't get to know how it all turns out. But we do get to choose how we show up today. This hour. This moment. And that's everything.

This is where healing happens: in the choosing.

What You Struggle With Can Become Your Strength

You might think your flaws disqualify you. But they can become the very ground where grace takes root.

What if the places where you fall short are the places where you most meet God?

The struggle itself—the resistance, the tiredness, the vulnerability—is not something to get over. It's part of the path. It teaches resilience. Humility. Depth.

Transformation doesn't come because we conquer our shadows. It comes when we stop pretending they're not there.

Find the Light and Reflect It

Look for people who are living the way you long to live—not as idols, but as mirrors.

Notice what resonates. Pay attention to what awakens hope in you. That's your inner compass. And when you're tempted to judge or compare, let it be a moment of reflection: *Is this something I need to learn? Or something I need to let go?*

We're all walking each other home. Let's not forget that.

The Practice of Showing Up

Sacred living isn't flashy. It's not about grand spiritual gestures. It's about the slow work of returning to your values, your integrity, your true self.

It's in the morning you choose silence over scrolling. It's in the conversation where you stay kind. It's in the decision to rest, to speak up, to walk away, to pray.

Discipline isn't punishment. It's devotion.

And when you commit to living intentionally, something shifts. You stop needing the world's permission to be at peace.

Let Go of the Outcome

One of the most liberating truths is this: You don't have to know how it ends.

You don't have to know if it'll all work out.

You just have to be willing to live in a way that matters now.

Let go of the fantasy of a perfect future. Instead, build a meaningful present.

Let your values shape your habits. Let your longing shape your path. Let your love shape your life.

Begin Again (And Keep Beginning)

No one's watching the clock. You haven't missed your chance.

So start where you are. With whatever honesty and humility you can gather. Not to prove anything. But because you're worth the effort.

If your soul is calling for change, don't wait until it's convenient.

Begin again.

And when you drift—and you will—come back again.

The sacred life isn't a straight line. It's a spiral of return.

Return to what matters.
Return to your breath.
Return to your Source.

The path is still open.
The invitation still stands.

Begin again.

Amen.

Afterword:
A Journey Just Beginning

If you have made it to these final pages, thank you. Not just for reading—but for walking alongside, for leaning in, for listening to the quiet whisper that perhaps brought you here in the first place.

This book began not with a grand vision, but with a longing. A longing for stillness in a noisy world. A longing for depth when so much feels shallow. A longing to remember what is sacred, and to live in a way that honours that memory.

And if that longing stirred in you too, then know this: you are not alone.

The reflections in these pages are not the end of the road. They are waymarks—stone cairns along a winding, sacred path. Paths like these are rarely linear. They spiral, they fold back, they lead us deeper into ourselves and closer to the Divine.

Sometimes we wander. Sometimes we forget. But always we are invited to return.

Return to the breath. Return to love. Return to the presence that has never truly left us.

If there is anything I hope remains with you, it is this: You are not behind. You are not too late. You are already on the path. And the path is holy.

May the words you've encountered here continue to live within you—not as rigid truths, but as gentle companions.

May you continue to seek not perfection, but presence. Not certainty, but wonder. Not answers, but the courage to ask better questions.

And may your life—however simple, however hidden—become a living prayer.

This is not the end. This is the hush before the next sacred step.

Keep walking. You're doing beautifully.

— Rob

Recommended Reading for the Journey

These books and authors have been chosen to companion you deeper into the themes of this work. Some will challenge you. Others will soothe you. All are offered as further steps along the sacred spiral.

Celtic Christianity & Contemplative Wisdom

Anam Cara – *John O'Donohue*
A beloved modern classic exploring soul friendship, presence, and the wild landscape of the inner life.

Sacred Earth, Sacred Soul – *John Philip Newell*
An invitation to rediscover the Celtic vision for justice, healing, and the sacredness of all life.

Listening for the Heartbeat of God – *J. Philip Newell*
A gateway into early Celtic Christian wisdom and its resonance with today's spiritual hunger.

Wisdom of the Celtic Saints – *Edward C. Sellner*
Short reflections on the lives and teachings of saints like Brigid, Cuthbert, and Aidan.

Modern Spiritual Formation & Soul Practice

The Eternal Current – *Aaron Niequist*
A practical guide to creating spiritual

rhythms that move beyond performance and into participation.

New Seeds of Contemplation – *Thomas Merton*
Mystical, poetic, and soul-deep, this is Merton at his most profound and accessible.

Everything Belongs – *Richard Rohr*
A compassionate invitation to see God in all things—including what we often reject in ourselves.

Inner Compass – *Margaret Silf*
Grounded in Ignatian practice, this book helps you listen to your life as a form of sacred guidance.

The Way of the Heart – *Henri Nouwen*
On solitude, silence, and prayer—simple practices that open the soul to God.

Deconstruction, Reimagining & Deepening Faith

With or Without God – *Gretta Vosper*
A challenging and freeing exploration of post-theistic spirituality within Christian frameworks.

Freeing Jesus – *Diana Butler Bass*
A personal and theological reimagining of Jesus through the stages of life.

Original Blessing – *Matthew Fox*
A powerful alternative to original sin theology—affirming humanity's inherent goodness and sacredness.

Poetry & the Language of the Soul

To Bless the Space Between Us – *John O'Donohue*
A rich collection of blessings for

thresholds, transitions, and everyday moments.

The Wild Edge of Sorrow – *Francis Weller*
An invitation to grieve deeply and ritually, with reverence for the soul's longing and loss.

Love Poems from God – *Daniel Ladinsky (translator)*
Mystical poems from Christian and Sufi saints like St. Francis, Rumi, and Hafiz—bridging devotion and wonder.

Let these words, like all sacred whispers, draw you deeper into presence, into love, and into the unfolding mystery of your own becoming.

A Blessing for the Journey

May you come now
to the place beyond striving—
where breath returns,
where grace gathers,
where the silence is not empty,
but full of presence.

And as you pause here,
you might begin to wonder...
what unfolds when there is nothing left to prove?

You don't need to go anywhere else to find peace.
You don't need to become someone else to be loved.

Even now, as you are,
you are already held.

May the old stories begin to fade—
the ones that said you had to earn it, fix it,
fight for it.
And may a new story rise in their place:
a story whispered in the dark
by the God who has never left your side.

Let your imagination drift...
to a life shaped by stillness,
a path walked in wonder,
a rhythm not of pressure, but of presence.

Because somewhere deep within you,
a knowing is awakening:
that what calls you forward
is not force,
but love.

So go gently.

Let the sacred spiral carry you onward.

And when you return—
to your morning, to your work, to your world—
may you carry with you the hush of holy ground,
the quiet confidence of the pilgrim,
and the soft, steady flame
of one who knows they are never alone.

Amen

Printed in Dunstable, United Kingdom